Our 6 His 7

Transformed by Sabbath Rest

Alisa Hope Wagner

Our 6 His 7

Transformed by Sabbath Rest

Our 6 His 7: Transformed by Sabbath Rest
Copyright @ 2015 by Alisa Hope Wagner.
All rights reserved. Marked Writers Publishing
www.alisahopewagner.com
Scriptures taken from multiple translations of the Bible.
Cover design by Alisa Hope Wagner
Author photo by Lori Stead of
www.wetsilver.com
Short story illustration by Albert Morales
ISBN-13:978-0692381175
ISBN-10:0692381171
BISAC: Religion/Christian Life/Spiritual Growth

Dedication

God—my Creator, Savior and Counselor

Daniel—my high school sweetheart and soul mate

Isaac—my first-born son

Levi—my brown-eyed boy

Karis Ruth—my cherished girl

Christina—my twin

I want to offer my sincerest gratitude to my family and friends who took time to read my initial drafts and offer me their valuable feedback. Your insights, suggestions and encouragement are added treasures to this book. I pray that your efforts on my behalf reap beautiful, eternal fruit. Thank you to Patti Coughlin, Cheryl Grundy, Susan Wood, Jennifer Smith, Pastor Dave Cotham, Cynthia Faulkner, Faith Newton and my husband, Daniel Wagner.

Forward

Pastor Bil Cornelius

Finally, we can claim peace from our constant human striving and enter into God's Promised Rest—a place of complete faith and complete surrender to the Lord. In Sabbath Rest, we relinquish our agendas, our expectations, and our desires, trusting that the Finished Work of Jesus Christ will resurrect our dreams in God's power, strength, and abundance!

Feelings of doubt, insecurity, and lack try to diminish our faith and prevent us from reaching our God-given destiny. Knowing that our efforts will always fall short of God's holy standard may cause us to bury our talents in the sand and book, *Our 6 His 7: Transformed by Sabbath Rest*, encourages us to live in the fullness of God's grace, knowing that the sacrifice of the cross transforms our human efforts into pleasing offerings to God. We give God our best, so He can do the rest!

Bil Cornelius is the founder and lead pastor of Church Unlimited in Corpus Christi, Texas. He can be seen hosting the Praise the Lord broadcast throughout the world on TBN. Bil is also a sought-

after speaker and church health and growth consultant and lives in Texas with his wife, Jessica, and their three children.

Table of Contents

INTRODUCTION I

CHAPTER 1 1

CHAPTER 2 9

CHAPTER 3 20

CHAPTER 4 31

CHAPTER 5 41

CHAPTER 6 55

CHAPTER 7 70

CHAPTER 8 78

CHAPTER 9 88

CHAPTER 10 97

CHAPTER 11 107

CHAPTER 12 118

CHAPTER 13 129

CHAPTER 14 140

CHAPTER 15 151

CHAPTER 16 160

CHAPTER 17 174

CHAPTER 18 187

CONCLUSION 195

Introduction

Enter God's Rest

We think of rest as a necessary inconvenience on humanity. In fact, in my speculative fiction books, the <u>Onoma Series</u>, the first book begins with my main character, Eve Pallue, coming out of a Sleeper—a machine which allows the user to encapsulate 8 hours of sleep into a little over 2 hours. Although our world has not yet produced a Sleeper, it is one of the prophecies of my book that my readers wish had been fulfilled. I pray it does not because getting more sleep is not the issue. It is our irritation with rest that signifies that we are overlooking something crucially important.

God is the Master Writer and nothing in the Bible is random or unimportant. Every chapter, every verse and every word has significance. In this book, I will tie four spiritual cords into a knot that can change your life. The chapters will overlap these truths until they are tightly woven into a reality that will set you on a path of God's supernatural power and strength, allowing you to finally rest from the daily grind of trying and striving but always coming up short.

The first cord of the knot is the number 6, which represents us and our work. It signifies the 6th day when people were created. Many times we believe this number is bad, but it is not. In Genesis 1.31, God saw what He had created on this day and it was "very good." Although we are a good creation, however, we will never be good enough. God is a holy God, and no matter how hard we try, we will never measure up to His perfect standard.

This is why God made day 7—a day of rest. The number 7 represents the second cord in the knot. God chose to rest, not that He needed it, but as an example to all of us. This is the day that God left empty and free for Jesus to do His work on the Cross. God declared the 7th day as holy, knowing it would be the supernatural elevator bringing all of creation (including us) onto His VIP level. This day is called the Sabbath, and we will learn why it not only represents physical rest but spiritual rest, as well.

Therefore, the third cord is Sabbath Rest. This rest is not simply a nap on a Sunday afternoon. Once our work is done, we rest in the fact that only Jesus can make our efforts pleasing to God. Without Jesus and what He accomplished on the Cross, we will work tirelessly and always be in lack and need. No matter how hard we labor, our efforts will fall short. Instead of continuously striving, we can take our work (our 6) and do as God did, and leave room for Jesus to do His work (His 7). After our work is done, we rest, so Jesus can do His work!

Finally, the fourth cord of this knot is the Blood of Jesus. We will discover through the chapters in this book that the Blood of Jesus Christ was poured out from day 7 and enveloped all of creation (day 1-6), making us and all the earth pleasing to God. The Blood of Jesus is the physical substance of grace released onto the earth. The Blood is God's Spirit of love and acceptance in the flesh extended to anyone who accepts Jesus as their Lord and Savior.

So here are the four cords of our knot: the number 6 (our work), the number 7 (His work), Sabbath Rest and the Blood of Jesus Christ. Each chapter of this book will intertwine these four cords together, so that you can finally understand why resting in Jesus will change your life.

Are you tired of feeling defeated? Do you lack victory in your life? Have you come to the end of yourself? Good. That's exactly where God wants you. Now you can let go of your striving and rest in the Finished Work of Jesus Christ. Read on. Your victory is at hand.

Chapter 1

David's Six Steps

"After the men who were carrying the Ark of the Lord had gone **six steps**, David sacrificed a bull and a fattened calf. And David danced before the Lord with all his might, wearing a priestly garment" (2 Samuel 6:13-14 NLT).

King David finally figured it out (read 2 Samuel 6). He had tried to carry the Ark of the Lord, God's holy presence, into the lives of God's Chosen People according to human strength. There was no sacrifice, there was no resting and one of David's men reached out his hand to hold the Ark because the oxen had stumbled. When Uzzah touched the Ark, he instantly died. The name *Uzzah* literally means *strength*. David was relying on human strength to accomplish his task of moving the Ark of the Lord instead of resting in God's strength, which is demonstrated through the sacrifice.

David became angry with himself and fearful of the Ark, and he was unwilling to take it back with him to Jerusalem (2 Samuel 6:6-10). And the man that David left the Ark with for 3 months was greatly blessed.

> *"And the ark of the LORD remained in the house of Obed-edom the Gittie three months, and the LORD blessed Obed-edom and all his household"* (2 Samuel 6:11 ESV).

David found himself in a conundrum: He wanted God's blessings given through the Ark, but he knew he couldn't acquire them in his own strength. David realized that he needed to rest in the sacrifice after his 6 steps of effort: *"After the men who were carrying the Ark of the Lord had gone **six steps**, David sacrificed a bull and a fattened calf"* (2 Samuel 6:13 NLT). David learned to rest in the sacrifice. He knew that only through a sacrifice could he possibly move God's blessings into his life because his strength alone would always fall short. After 6 steps, David made sure that 2 animals were sacrificed. I know that the word, "blood," leaves many people with bad images, but the spilled Blood of sacrifice is amazingly beautiful when considered outside of our cultural portrayal of it.

The spilled Blood depicts atonement—everything being made right before the eyes of our holy God. So when we imagine King David sacrificing the animals after 6 steps, we gain a redemptive image of human effort being washed by the Blood of atonement. And the path that King David took to Zion, carrying the presence of the Lord, is the same path we walk today. Christians carry in themselves the presence of the Ark of Lord, the Holy Spirit. As we walk our path to our heavenly Zion, our steps—our human efforts—will fall short of God's perfect standard. In fact, God does not like it when we rely on anything other than Him to be the saving grace in all areas of our lives. According to Jeremiah, God views our reliance on our own strength as turning our hearts away from Him.

> "This is what the Lord says: 'Cursed are those who put their trust in mere humans, who rely on human strength and turn their hearts away from the Lord'" (Jeremiah 17:5 NLT).

But when we take the 6 steps of our human effort, knowing the end result will have to come from God, we can finally enter into His Rest because our hearts are centered on Him. We can rest in the atoning Blood of Jesus Christ, and our actions will be accepted by the Lord and filled with His strength, power and blessing. It is not about our strength; it is about the sacrifice of the Great Lamb of God. It's about giving God our 6 steps, and resting in the 7th step—the sacrifice of Jesus Christ. Only God's 7 will make our 6 pleasing to a holy God.

David did something amazing on his second attempt to bring the Ark of the Lord into Jerusalem—he danced! He stripped himself of his royal robes and clad himself with a linen ephod, the same ephod the priests wear. David was exposed and vulnerable before the Lord, and all of God's people experienced David's joy. He was so exuberant in his exaltations to the Lord, that his wife, Michal, criticized him, making fun of his childlike praise. Her judgment would cause her to miss out on the blessing of the Lord that David passed onto his family. David's anger and fear were transformed into dancing because of the sacrifice. The Bible says that people are the New Testament *"royal priesthood" (1 Peter 2:9)*. Like David, we need to shed ourselves of our human titles, and clad ourselves with our priestly ephod. We can give God the 6 steps of human effort, knowing that the sacrifice of Jesus will make our work for the Lord pleasing. By all means, we should dance with David's exuberance because we can claim God's blessings in our lives by the Blood of Jesus shed for our forgiveness and acceptance.

We will all come to the point in our lives when we realize that our efforts aren't good enough. In fact, we may even come to the conclusion that our efforts are actually working against us. We strive and strive to accomplish God's will for our lives, but we always fall short. Instead of getting ahead, we feel like we keep messing up, sabotaging the very desires that God instilled in us. Every time we build up our strength, it only gets stripped away again. We are not resting in the Sabbath Rest that God ordained for us. The Sabbath Rest is not simply a day in a week; it is a lifestyle. It is choosing to rest in the Finished Work of Jesus Christ on the Cross. Today we don't have to sacrifice animals to atone for our work because the ministry of Jesus Christ is continually spilling the Blood of atonement on our efforts for the Lord.

Yes, Blood does sound strange at first, but when we understand the full weight of what Jesus' Blood means for our lives, we will embrace the Blood of Christ above all else. The Blood of Jesus not only forgives us, but it makes our steps of pleasing, righteous and acceptable to God. In later chapters, I'm going to reveal what the Holy Spirit has shown me about the Blood of Christ and how it has created the Sabbath Rest that we can choose to enter into today. Just like you, I would read people's words about the Blood and question why it was so important. I would read the Bible and wonder about all the Sacrificial Blood spilled on the altar. What seemed messy and bizarre to me at first has now become a precious image of redemption and salvation.

> *"Let us look steadfastly to the blood of Christ, and see how precious that blood is*

to God, which, having been shed for our salvation, has set the grace of repentance before the whole world." – Clement of Rome

I've read through the Bible many times, and the portions of the splattering Blood always threw me off. Finally, one day I determined myself to meditate on one of the gruesome images from the Old Testament of Blood being splattered. I imagined myself standing next to the altar as the priest sprinkled the Blood. I felt the Blood spray across my face and arms. Instead of feeling disgusted, however, I felt something beautiful. This beauty was not of this world or Hollywood's depiction. It was of something higher and grander that I couldn't explain it, which is why I set my heart to understand it. This Blood was the physical form of grace being splashed onto me.

Personal Application

1. Has God ever asked you to do something that scared you or seemed impossible?

2. Are you in a situation right now where you are trying to fix something or make something happen, but nothing you do seems to work?

3. How can you give the situation to God because there is nothing else that you can offer? How can you let go of your human striving and trust the situation to the hands of the Father?

Today, stop striving to achieve something only God can do. Trust God and let go of control, resting your situation in the Blood of Jesus Christ. Jesus will redeem your situation. Jesus will accomplish what you can't in all your striving. Learn to rest in the sacrifice of the Cross. Learn to abide in the Finished Work of Jesus

"Father, I give you all control today. I'm tired of striving. I'm tired of never seeing the results I want from all my efforts. I trust that You can do

the impossible. I choose to rest in You. I give you all control, and I will enjoy this day that You have given me without worry and without stress. I believe the sacrifice of Jesus on the Cross can redeem my work, my plans and my situation. I pray this in Jesus' name, amen."

Chapter 2

The First Miracle

"On the third day a wedding took place at Cana in Galilee. Jesus' mother was there, and Jesus and his disciples had also been invited to the wedding" (John 2:1-2 NIV).

Whenever we see something occurring for the first time in the Bible, there is a significant statement that God is making. The first sacrifice of an animal covered Adam and Eve's shame (foreshadowing the process of redemption). The first rainbow in the sky promised a second chance (symbolizing the ability for second chances). The first Passover protected the homes marked by the lamb's blood (establishing the covenant of the Lamb's Blood). Every *first* found in the Bible is making a statement, saying, "Look at me! I'm different and special! God is doing something new!"

Jesus' first public miracle found in the second chapter of the Book of John is powerful because it sets the stage for why Jesus has come to the earth. He didn't heal someone. He didn't multiply dinner for 5,000 plus people. He didn't bring someone back from the dead. He simply helped a friend in a situation that would have brought shame on his family, and we'll discover that Jesus has a special knack for covering our shame.

People in Jesus' time didn't have the distractions that we are bombarded with today, so when something big happened—like a birth of a child, death of a loved one or a marriage of a young couple—everyone stopped what they were doing and involved themselves in the joy and sorrow of others for days or even weeks. Jesus has just begun His public ministry when He attends the wedding in Cana. The person getting married has to be related to Jesus or at least a friend of the family for Jesus to be invited. And the fact that Jesus' mother takes a personal effort to prevent shame from being brought onto the family shows that she cares deeply about the couple.

> *"When the wine was gone, Jesus' mother said to him, 'They have no more wine.' 'Woman, why do you involve me?' Jesus replied. 'My hour has not yet come.' His mother said to the servants, 'Do whatever he tells you'" (John 2:3-5 NIV).*

In a literal sense, wine was an important staple, like bread and oil, especially in an area and time when water could be scarce. If the wedding celebration ran out of wine, the guests would have nothing to drink with their meal. Someone could fetch and serve water, but that would bring further embarrassment to the wedding party because wine was the expected drink at joyous occasions. I'm sure when the family planned the wedding, they hoped that the wine they served would last the several days of celebration. But in their human effort and with their limited resources, they could only bring to the feast the amount of wine that was feasible for them, which obviously ran dry.

The wedding feast is all out of wine and God is trying to tell us something about Jesus. Jesus' mother runs to Him and explains the situation. And Jesus says in a loving first-born tone, *"Dear woman, why do you involve me? My time has not yet come" (John 2:4 NIV).* Mary does what any good mother would do and ignores her Son's nonresponsive comment, telling the servants to do whatever Jesus says. She knows her Son can fix the problem because, like all of us, the people closest to us will experience our giftedness and abilities first. A beautiful mesh of wills occurs, and God allows Mary to have her way, incorporating her efforts of redeeming the wedding ceremony into the beautiful symbolic demonstration of Jesus' redemption for all God's Children: Jesus becomes the 7 to our 6.

We always assume that when Jesus told His mother that His time had not yet come that He was referring to His public ministry, but there is a deeper revelation to be found. What if the first public miracle of Jesus' ministry symbolically represents the reason for His ministry? The Bible has several layers of revelation in every verse, and we must dig a little deeper to get the treasure-trove of meaning just beneath the surface. Mary wanted Jesus to produce wine for a wedding feast that had run dry, but maybe Jesus' eyes were set on another wedding feast— The Wedding Banquet that the Father was preparing in His Kingdom for His Son and His Son's bride, the Church: *"The kingdom of heaven is like a king who prepared a wedding banquet for his son" (Matthew 22:2 NIV).* Jesus knew the Wine (His Blood) for this wedding feast was not yet ready to be poured out.

We find that at the Last Supper Jesus compared His body to bread: "While they were eating, Jesus took bread, and when he had given thanks, he broke it and gave it to his disciples, saying, *'Take and eat; this is my body'" (Matthew 26:26 NIV).* And He compared His Blood to wine: *"Then he took a cup, and when he had given thanks, he gave it to them, saying, 'Drink from it, all of you. This is my blood of the covenant, which is poured out for many for the forgiveness of sins'" (Matthew 26:27-28 NIV).* His body is important because it symbolizes that He left His glory, becoming flesh just like humanity. It is also important because it is the natural encasement for His Blood. His body, in effect, would be broken in the natural world, allowing the supernatural life-essence of His salvation to cover the shame of the earth. He would restore on the 7th day the glory that was stolen on the 6th.

The wine is all gone at the wedding feast, and Jesus symbolically replenishes it through the supernatural work of His redemption, concealing the shame of the wedding party. Jesus told His mother that it was not time to spill His Blood, but He allowed His first miracle to be a beautiful whisper of the redemption to come.

> *"Instead, he gave up his divine privileges; he took the humble position of a slave and was born as a human being..." (Philippians 2:7 NLT).*

In our lives, we too will run dry. We will give God all of our human efforts, but we will always come up short. As we fill our day with the busyness of layers upon layers of responsibility, we wonder in the quiet moments of the night if our efforts truly matter. We question why everything is so difficult, why our efforts fall short, why our work creates more lack and why we are not living in victory. And as we consume ourselves with worry and confusion, God softly wills us to recognize the answer that He has already set in place. The 7th day is His answer.

The 7th day is His gift to us. The 7th day is when God rested, knowing that Jesus will spill His Blood to reconcile all the striving in this world and our lives. David knew to sacrifice the animals after the 6th step because he understood the importance of the 7th step of atonement and redemption. Our work will never be good enough, which is why we must rest in the Finished Work of Jesus.

During the years I waited for God to fulfill His promises to me, I told Him so many times, "But I'm a workhorse, God! Tell me to do something, and I'll do it. But all this waiting is driving me crazy!" If it were a wedding feast for my family, I would have raced around the city like a madwoman trying to find wine. And if I didn't have any money, I would have sold something valuable or given up my life savings in order to save the wedding from shame. I would have given up everything for the leftover wine that some vendor was saving for a desperate woman like me.

And in my efforts to redeem the wedding myself, I not only would have failed miserably, I would have also circumvented God's miracle through Jesus Christ and His Rest. Even the great Christian thinker, Oswald Chambers, confides that learning to wait is one the biggest struggles we face: *"One of the greatest strains in life is the strain of waiting for God."* But the power of waiting on God's timing and resting in His strength will transform our lives if we would only let it.

God doesn't want us to redeem a situation in our human efforts when it obviously requires a miracle. Maybe we would have a lot more miracles in our world today if Christians stopped trying to do everything in our own strength. We show an immense lack of belief in God when we pull the reigns from His hands. God is not for a single second surprised by our need and our lack. He allowed it, so we can learn to rely on Him. We waste our time and energy, trying to fix things that only God can fix through the Finished Work of Jesus Christ. It took me so long to figure this out. God doesn't want me running around trying to solve every problem. He wants me to enter into His Sabbath Rest and wait for Him to transform my lack, my need, my worry, my confusion and my shame into His glorious abundance. As a writer, I think back to all the time I wasted trying to get my first book published, and I could have spent that time enjoying God's presence, getting to know Him more and more.

Through the years, I was so focused on being a published writer—wondering every day if this would be the day that my book would be picked up by a publisher. But the days turned to months and the months turned to years—almost 8 years to be exact! I wish I could go back and just enjoy each day with Him and not worry about when He was going to fulfill His promises to me. I would have diligently worked at the tasks He called me to each day and waited patiently in His Rest for the fulfillment of His promises. If I had entered in Sabbath Rest earlier and truly given God the situation, I would have saved myself years of frustration.

Sabbath is a translation of a Hebrew word that literally means "covering," which we will discuss in later chapters. Sabbath is symbolic of atoning or covering shame. So when we view the 7th Day of rest, we can imagine a great atoning blanket, covering all of creation that was corrupted by the blessing and burden of free will. We know that Jesus is eternal and that He dwells outside of time because the Bible states that all of creation was made through Him.

> *"In the beginning the Word already existed. The Word was with God, and the Word was God. He existed in the beginning with God. God created everything through him, and nothing was created except through him" (John 1:1-3 NLT).*

However, we know that Jesus had to enter into God's creation during the week of its formation. We know that He ate with His disciples, walked down dirt paths and forged relationships with

His people. So if Jesus didn't enter creation in days 1-6, we must surmise that He entered on day 7. And that's why Jesus claimed that He was the Lord over Sabbath: *"For the Son of Man is Lord, even over the Sabbath!" (Matthew 12:8 NLT)*. Therefore, we can learn by God's example on the 7th day of creation and rest. God doesn't need rest, but He lovingly illustrated the most amazing process: After we create our 6 for God, we must rest in the Sabbath of Jesus, so He can transform our hearts, minds, families, efforts and situations with the creative power of His Finished Work.

> *"Rely on the certainty of God's redemptive power, and He will create His own life in people."* – Oswald Chambers

Personal Application

1. Have you felt like you worked so hard only to come up short? Did you feel embarrassment towards what others thought of you or resentment towards God?

2. Considering the wedding feast and the wine that ran dry, do you now think that God may have allowed you to come to the end of yourself? Did you stand your ground and believe for a miracle or did you leave the scene filled with doubt and despair?

3. Does knowing that God will purposefully lead you into lack, so He can provide for you in His abundance encourage you to remain faithful, trusting that God will come through?

Remember that God wants to pour His abundance into your life, but you must trust the process and cling tightly to belief even when every circumstance in your life declares that you are in trouble. God wants you to reach passed your limitations and grab unto His supernatural provision. Don't allow your mind and spirit to worry or doubt. Rather, stand firm and wait for God to provide.

"Father, I believe that You are more than capable of transforming my lack into Your abundance. I realize that Jesus has already saved me from eternal separation from You, so I can trust You with the problems I face in this fleeting life. I give You my emptiness and lack, trusting that You will fill that void and need with Your best. I pray this in Jesus' name, amen."

Chapter 3

The Six Jars

"Nearby stood six stone water jars, the kind used by the Jews for ceremonial washing, each holding from twenty to thirty gallons" (John 2:6 NIV).

At the wedding feast in Cana, the hosts were out of wine (read John 2:1-11). There was nothing to be done in the natural, so Mary went straight to the source that could produce the supernatural, Jesus. The Bible states that there were 6 large jars (each able to hold up to 20-30 gallons of water) that were used for the Jewish ceremonial washing. The people of the day would pour the water over each hand, and the water mixed with their dirty hands would pour onto the earth. Jesus told the servants to fill the jugs to the brim with water, but this time the water would not be poured back out for literal cleansing; rather, it would represent wine for our supernatural cleansing poured out through Christ.

People became ceremonially unclean by touching the normal, everyday objects that they used for work, so they would have to cleanse themselves of all the natural elements before they could eat. The dirt from working the ground, shepherding the heard, cleaning the home and caring for infants would be caked on the hands of God's Children. It's no coincidence that there happened to be 6 jars nearby at the wedding feast because 6 symbolizes human effort. The jars paint an image of our 6 being transformed by the power of Jesus' 7 as we rest in Him.

> "Jesus said to the servants, 'Fill the jars with water'; so they filled them to the brim. Then he told them, 'Now draw some out and take it to the master of the banquet'" (John 2:7-8 NIV).

The 6 jars used to wash the dirt of human effort become containers for Jesus to perform a miracle. One conclusion from this miracle is that our time of striving to be cleansed has finally ended because Jesus' Finished Work on the Cross cleanses us completely and eternally. Another conclusion is that the blood or (wine) of Christ would finally quench our thirst for the Living Water of God. Jesus depicts a beautiful picture of Living Water (God) in the flesh (wine) poured out for all to drink. The water becomes the best wine, satisfying our thirst for

Emmanuel, God with Us, and giving us a spring of eternal life.

> *"But those who drink the water I give will never be thirsty again. It becomes a fresh, bubbling spring within them, giving them eternal life"* (John 4:14 NLT).

Not only is the reputation of the wedding family saved, but the wedding will be forever blessed by the mark of supernatural provision from God. In order to have the supernatural power of Jesus poured out on us, we have to humbly admit our need. We live in a society where the focus is on human strength—our ability, our resources, our talents, our strength, our position, our platform, our connections—and we are robbing ourselves of the supernatural rest and move of God in our lives. As Jesus came closer and closer to His time on the Cross, He began to emphasize taking the lowest place to His disciples more and more.

> *"But when you are invited, take the lowest place, so that when your host comes, he will say to you, 'Friend, move up to a better place.' Then you will be honored in the presence of all the other guests"* (Luke 14:10 NIV).

We will all come to that point in our lives where we realize we don't have what it takes to fulfill God's promises. It might take a while, and we may wind up giving God a bunch of 6's in the process; but even in our efforts done at the expense of God's rest, we will always find ourselves lacking. But this does not surprise God. He needs us to get to the place of complete drought in our own efforts, so when He does unleash His promises in our lives, we won't give people the bullet list of what "we did" to achieve our dreams. We can do absolutely nothing to earn God's promises—even the filthy rags of effort we offer God are received by grace.

> "All of us have become like one who is unclean, and all our righteous acts are like filthy rags; we all shrivel up like a leaf, and like the wind our sins sweep us away" (Isaiah 64:6 NIV).

We must keep our eyes on Jesus. His work of grace is our only hope of living a life with a true purpose that is rooted in eternity. Our busyness will never replace a life that has eternal value, and we must not allow ourselves to rely on our self-effort, forfeiting the transforming work of Jesus. When we turn our eyes from Jesus and His Redeeming Work on the Cross, we will try to do things in our own time and effort beyond the 6 that God requires of us. We will start to overwork ourselves, leaving the Sabbath Rest of God. When we leave God's rest, we step into the spirit of the flesh and the tripled 6 of the antichrist.

It's shocking when we read that statement: "tripled 6 of the antichrist." And we would never believe that our efforts could be against Christ, but if we are not obedient to His timing and patiently waiting in His Sabbath Rest, that is exactly what we are doing—moving in a spirit without Christ, trying to accomplish His promises by our own efforts. And that is what happened to Cain when he made his offering to God. Cain gave God the fruit of the ground. The earth also represents our flesh, human effort and the natural world. That is why God cursed the snake to eat from the dust of the earth because Satan would be devouring the flesh (selfish will) of every generation throughout time. Cain gave God the fruit of his natural efforts without relying on the sacrifice of the Lamb.

> *"Cursed are you above all livestock and all wild animals! You will crawl on your belly and you will eat dust all the days of your life" (Genesis 3:14 NIV).*

When God received Cain's offering, He said, *"Why are you angry? Why is your face downcast? If you do what is right, will you not be accepted? But if you do not do what is right, sin is crouching at your door; it desires to have you, but you must rule over it" (Genesis 4:6-7 NIV).* God knew that Cain gave the fruits of his own self-efforts because they didn't have the mark of sacrifice on them. The offering may look pleasing to us, but God examines the motives found in our heart and mind (Jeremiah 17:10). And since Satan is able to devour any fruit that is given in the flesh and not in the sacrifice, we can be sure that Satan's teeth marks are all over them. That is why Satan is so consumed with keeping our culture and this generation so busy. He wants us distracted with all of our own efforts, so we don't rely on the Finished Work of Jesus on the Cross. Satan makes waiting have a bad taste in our mouths, so we avoid God's preordained Sabbath Rest. But Satan's time of consuming our efforts ends when we realize our work will never please God without the Finished Work of Christ.

What is so scary is not that Cain's offering was given out of the efforts of his flesh; rather, it was a sanctioned offering given to God, and Cain was clueless of why God was not pleased with it. I remember when I volunteered in the women's ministry at my church. I was doing all these amazing things for God; however, I was becoming overworked and I started holding a grudge. I started to document all the time I was spending "doing ministry," and I realized that I was sacrificing time with my family. I had little kids at this time, and God always leads mothers with small children gently. Instead of finding rest in God, I had allowed my public ministry to become an idol in my life, and much of my security was placed in my work.

"He tends his flock like a shepherd: He gathers the lambs in his arms and carries them close to his heart; he gently leads those that have young" (Isaiah 40:11 NIV).

I went to God with my documented timeline and questioned how He could let ministry run me dry, and I felt Him sternly look down at me and say, "I never asked you to do any of that." I was so shocked. I thought ministry was an automatic obedience checkmark for God. I had started in ministry by obedience, but I ignored God when He started prompting me to let go and stay home for a season. Instead of listening to God, I amped up my efforts and started offering a bunch of my 6's. I didn't notice God's promptings because I was so wrapped up in my efforts and the security they brought me. It wasn't until I had run dry that I revealed to God my need. Although public ministry was in my heart, it was not yet God's time for me. I didn't know it yet, but He was about to bring me into the wilderness, so I could grow a personal ministry with the Lord first.

On the contrary, Abel gave the sacrifice of the Lamb, and His offering was pleasing to the Lord. But we must never think that Abel's sacrifice was easy. To be sure he had to care for the lamb, feed it and protect it. Most scholars believe that if it weren't for human effort, sheep would be extinct by now because they are so helpless.

Abel had to give God years of his 6—taking the lamb to the meadows for food, bringing it down to the stream for water, taking out thorns from his hoof and protecting it from the sharp claws of the bears and wolves. But when it came time to offer his work, he sacrificed the lamb, knowing that it was only through the Blood of Sacrifice that his efforts would be pleasing to the Lord.

Abel gave God his 6 and waited in Sabbath Rest, relying on Jesus to give His 7. Abel's efforts were seeded in the spirit because he kept his focus on the Sacrificial Lamb. His motives were centered on the truth that none of his efforts for God would be pleasing without the Blood of the Lamb covering them. We will never please God unless our efforts wait with great anticipation and joyous excitement of the supernatural move of God in them. I love how Corrie ten Boom identifies the "Ministry of Jesus" in our work. She explains that without the ministry of Jesus flowing in our lives, our efforts will run us ragged! *"Trying to do the Lord's work in your own strength is the most confusing, exhausting, and tedious of all work. But when you are filled with the Holy Spirit, then the ministry of Jesus just flows out of you."*

That is why Jesus' first miracle is so important: it explains the reason for His coming. He came into this earth to bring the New Wine of His Salvation by fulfilling the promise for a Messiah found in the Old Testament. The Bible states that all of our works are like filthy rags; so no matter the efforts we offer to God, they will never be good enough. We can only give God a 6, but because of His holiness, He can only receive a perfect and complete 7. God has a holy standard, but He is also the personification of love. He knows that we will fall short of His glory, so He sent Himself into this earth to achieve what we couldn't do on our own— offering His perfect life, so our efforts could be complete in Him. Jesus came to this earth so that His supernatural 7 could be given freely to a people who could only produce a 6. It is by grace found on the Cross that our human efforts are made perfect and pleasing to God.

> *"Every story of conversion is a story of blessed defeat."* – C.S. Lewis

Personal Application

1 Are there any areas in your life that you have been multiplying your own efforts instead of resting in the Finished Work of Jesus on the Cross?

2. Even when something looks good it doesn't mean it is being done in accordance with God's will. Is there something in your life that looks pleasant, but really it is being committed in disobedience?

3. Have you surrendered all of your human effort to God? Are there things in your life that God does not have complete authority over?

Human striving without the anointing of the Holy Spirit may be working against God's plan for your life. Every effort you make is wasted unless it is covered by the Blood of Jesus and connected to His Vine. Only through Jesus will your efforts be pleasing to the Father. You can give God all your efforts, but when your work falls short, you must rest in the Sabbath of Jesus.

"God, I know that only You can take my measly efforts and make them into great demonstrations of Your glory and grace. I give You all the work of my hands. I want the Blood of Jesus to cover over my offerings to You, so they can be pleasing in Your eyes. If there is anything in my life that is not redeemed by the Finished Work of Jesus, please let me know. Help me to place all my work in Your Sabbath Rest. I pray this in Jesus' name, amen."

Chapter 4

Need for Numbers

"All Scripture is inspired by God and is useful to teach us what is true and to make us realize what is wrong in our lives. It corrects us when we are wrong and teaches us to do what is right" (2 Timothy 3:16 NLT).

Numbers have meaning in the Bible. All good writers know that we don't add details into a book unless they are important. God is the Master Writer and nothing in the Bible is superfluous—everything has a meaning if we are only willing to dig for it. The number 6 is symbolic of human nature and our efforts. We were created on the 6th day (Genesis 1:27-31). We work 6 days out of the week (Exodus 34:21). The land was to be cultivated 6 years before a year of rest (Exodus 23:10-11). The Children of God wandering the wilderness had to gather double the manna on the 6th day, so they could rest on the 7th (Exodus 16:22).

The number 6 represents our efforts, our flesh, our human nature and the natural world. God created the animals, seed-bearing plants and humans on the 6th day. The family hosting the wedding feast from Jesus' first miracle had done everything in their power (their 6) to honor the guests who were celebrating the covenant of marriage with them, but they still had lack. Their 6 was incomplete.

There is nothing inherently wrong with the number 6. However, it is when we rely on our 6 alone that major problems occur. The number of the antichrist is 666. Anything repeated 3 times is showing emphasis and fulfillment in and of itself. For example, when the seraphim cry out, *"**Holy, holy, holy** is the LORD Almighty; the whole earth is full of his glory" (Isaiah 6:3 NIV)*, there is a demonstration of completion of God's holiness. The number 3 represents our Triune God who is complete within Himself as the Father (Creator), Son (Savior) and Holy Spirit (Counselor).

However, when we focus on our efforts alone and disregard the supernatural power and presence of the Lord; our 6 triples, becoming the emphasis, and we fall into the trap of self-reliance. Instead, we must give our efforts in accordance with God's will and wait on His supernatural intervention in our lives and situations. We wouldn't want to waste our efforts on constantly coming up short with our

6's. As we will see, Jesus' 7 is worth the wait and the only way our 6 will find redemption. Our efforts will never be pleasing to the Father, which is why we need the covenant of the Pierced Lamb of God.

> *"The Lord is good to those whose hope is in him, to the one who seeks him; it is good to wait quietly for the salvation of the Lord" (Lamentations 3:25-26 NIV).*

The wine running out at the wedding feast parallels what is happening to Israel and God's Chosen people at the time Jesus began His ministry. The Old Testament ended in Malachi with promises of the Messiah and yet there is 400 years of oppressive spiritual drought. By the time John the Baptist begins to prepare the way for the Lord, the Israelites were all out of the revelation wine of God's promises. Their eager expectation for the Son of David to come and rescue them from their oppressors to establish a new kingdom was all dried up. Many of God's Children got tired of waiting and started focusing on producing their own 6's as counterfeits to what only Jesus could do.

In fact, the true nature of the Messiah as written in the Scriptures was completely barren. God was establishing His Kingdom on earth through the sacrifice of Jesus on the Cross, which would bring Jews and Gentiles alike back into the family of God through grace. But the religious leaders were not sensitive to God's Kingdom because they were too busy trying to establish their own kingdoms with their limited understanding. They were wrapped up in multiplying their 6's, instead of crying out and waiting for God's 7. The religious leaders had become blind to the things of God.

> *"When evening comes, you say, 'It will be fair weather, for the sky is red,' and in the morning, 'Today it will be stormy, for the sky is red and overcast.' You know how to interpret the appearance of the sky, but you cannot interpret the signs of the times" (Matthew 16:2-3 NIV).*

The religious leaders seemed to find ways to accuse Jesus and find fault in His actions. Jesus had already fed the 5,000 and performed many other miracles, but they still came to Him, insisting on seeing a sign from heaven. They had to have known that Jesus was doing supernatural work or else they wouldn't have bothered to find Jesus and question Him. They were not only blind to the signs of the time, they were also trying to work against them. They had built up and fortified their 6's, yet they were as hollow as tombs. They knew if anything shook their current establishments too hard, they would crumble to the ground. But that is precisely what God was about to do—He was shaking heaven and earth to expose the 6's that were not resting in the Sabbath of Jesus.

"At that time his voice shook the earth, but now he has promised, 'Once more I will shake not only the earth but also the heavens.' The words 'once more' indicate the removing of what can be shaken— that is, created things—so that what cannot be shaken may remain (Hebrews 12:26-27 NIV).

God uses this wedding feast and Mary's concern for the wedding party as an illustration of His concern for His people. And just like Mary, God knew He could count on Jesus to fulfill the need for new wine. God allowed His chosen people to come to the end of their human effort as a way to highlight their need for a Savior.

They needed to recognize that they in their own strength were unable to please the Father without a mediator and the covenant of His Blood. They had to experience the devastating spiritual lack they had without the supernatural intervention of God. They kept trying to fulfill God's promises in their own strength, which caused them to stop focusing on God and turn to relying on the efforts of people. They waited for 400 years for God to move, but they finally gave up waiting for the Master, and they began to preoccupy themselves with things of this world. The old wine had finally run dry, and the servants were no longer about their Master's business.

"Therefore keep watch, because you do not know on what day your Lord will come. But understand this: If the owner of the house had known at what time of night the thief was coming, he would have kept watch and would not have let his house be broken into. So you also must be ready, because the Son of Man will come at an hour when you do not expect him" (Matthew 24:42-44 NIV).

The saddest part of this story is that many of the religious leaders who had read the promises of the Messiah would not recognize Jesus as the Savior. They had become so established and comfortable in their efforts of 6 that their old wines skins couldn't contain the new wine of Christ. The religious leaders questioned Jesus' unorthodox methods, experiencing first hand that He was coming with power and purpose beyond the norms they were accustomed to. It was obvious to them that Jesus wasn't trapped by the parameters of human effort. Jesus didn't act the part of the established religious leaders with their magnified and multiplied 6's. They didn't know it, but Jesus was the 7 that they had long forgotten about.

"Neither do people pour new wine into old wineskins. If they do, the skins will burst; the wine will run out and the wineskins will be ruined. No, they pour new wine

into new wineskins, and both are preserved" (Matthew 9:17 NIV).

Our public ministry for the Lord must always rest in the Sabbath. When we start to burden people in our sphere of influence with notions of self-focus—our talents, our strengths, our platforms, our abilities, etc.—we limit (or even worse) halt the supernatural power of Jesus' atoning work! Satan loves to make God's people take their focus off of Jesus and His Sabbath Rest, willing us to put our gaze on the work of our flesh.

Like I said earlier, there is nothing wrong with our efforts of 6; but when we feel that we've done everything we can do out of obedience, we must enter into our Sabbath Rest. A serious problem that occurs in our society today is that we feel entitled to always be in a season of plenty. We don't like to experience a time of lack.

As we make our journey to attaining the promises that God has for us, we will most definitely discover how much we are lacking. All God's promises for us are impossible without the atoning work of the Sabbath—they will all take a super amount of reliance on God's faithfulness. We will always experience a serious time of lack just before God moves on our behalf. Just like at the wedding feast, they had to completely run out of wine before Jesus performed His miracle. Many times we get anxious in that time of lack and we start trying to fix the situation ourselves, but we need to stop. The emptier we feel and the emptier our situation, the more Jesus can pour out His abundance.

Don't question the lack. Every person in the Bible experienced a great lack before God moved. This is not only a normal part of the process; it is a crucial part. I wish I would have known this so long ago. Instead of constantly striving in my own effort and grumbling to God about my lack, I would have entered into His Sabbath Rest and waited in the joy and peace of His timing, knowing that He is a faithful God.

> *"I do know that waiting on God requires the willingness to bear uncertainty, to carry within oneself the unanswered question, lifting the heart to God about it whenever it intrudes upon one's thoughts."* – Elisabeth Elliot

Personal Application

1. Is your life and service to the Lord built on taking the last seat and allowing God to shine in your life through your obedience?

2. Have you ever been caught up in the world's pressure to build yourself up in order to make a mark in your culture or do you trust God to rise up in your situation?

3. Did you know that you will come to a point in life when there is nothing else you can do to achieve your promises except wait on God?

God plants your promises in a land that you will never be able to enter without His supernatural intervention. You will either have to claim a lesser promise in your own strength or trust God for His best promise and wait on Him. God's promises will come to fruition if He promised them, but they will have to die in the natural first, so He can resurrect them in the supernatural.

"God, help me to allow my dreams to die, so You can resurrect them in Your supernatural power. Show me how to abide in the Sabbath Rest that Jesus died to give me. I don't want to achieve lesser dreams in my own strength. I want the best dreams that You have promised me. Help me to wait and trust in You. I pray this in Jesus' name, amen."

Chapter 5

All Things New

*"And he who was seated on the throne said, 'Behold, I am making **all things new**.' Also he said, 'Write this down, for these words are trustworthy and true'" (Revelation 21:5 ESV).*

There's very little written about Jesus' childhood, except for His birth (found in all four Gospels) and the time when he was 13 years old and He decided to stay back at the Temple while His parents went home without Him (every parents' nightmare) (Luke 2:41-51). However, at the age of 30, Jesus responds to the Voice in the Wilderness. John the Baptist is taking a huge step of faith by proclaiming that the Kingdom of Heaven is near.

This statement was a massive leap of faith because it had been over 400 years since the last prophecies of Christ in the Book of Malachi. Malachi writes in his final chapter and the last book of the Old Testament: *"But for you who fear* *my name, the **Sun of Righteousness** will rise with healing in his wings. And you will go free, leaping with joy like calves let out to pasture"* (Malachi 4:2 NLT). Jesus is the Great Light, shining in the hearts of this world, and He is about to pierce the darkness with His forgiveness, mercy and grace; but people would have to wait for 400 years.

> *"For God, who said, 'Let light shine out of darkness,' made his light shine in our hearts to give us the light of the knowledge of God's glory displayed in the face of Christ"* (2 Corinthians 4:6 NIV).

At the time of Malachi's final prophesy, God's Chosen People had returned to Jerusalem, had rebuilt their Temple and had been living in their Promised Land for approximately 100 years, but they were already showing signs of unfaithfulness to God. It became keenly evident that God's Children would bankrupt in their efforts to serve Him once more, but God would not let the story end in devastation again. Out of His great love for us, He would finally make His supernatural move on the earth. God had to let His Chosen people run out of the Old Wine and feel the dryness of their own efforts, so He could supply them with His miraculous abundance. They needed to give God their 6 of human effort, so He could unleash the 7 of the Sabbath Rest found in Jesus.

God gave His People the standard of His perfect 7 long before in the laws of Moses on Mount Sinai, and the people foolishly thought that they could fulfill His 7 without the help of a mediator. They told Moses, *"We will do everything the Lord has said" (Exodus 19:8 NIV)*. Moses brought their reply to God; and while God listed in detail His standard of holiness to Moses on the mountain, the people got tired of waiting and multiplied their 6's. It took them no time at all to stop relying on the Lord and start focusing on their own efforts. Aaron made a golden calf (from the treasure that God had given them), and God's people began to worship it. After God had carried them out of slavery, provided for them in the wilderness and made a supernatural covenant with them at the First Passover with the blood of the sacrificed lamb, they still defaulted back into the spirit of the flesh.

> *"You yourselves have seen what I did in Egypt, and how I carried you on eagle's wings and brought you to myself. Now if you obey me fully and keep my covenant, then out of all the nations you will be my treasured possession. Although the whole earth is mine, you will be for me a kingdom of priests and a holy nation. These are the words you are to speak to the Israelites (Exodus 19:4-6 NIV).*

Since the People of God left their time of waiting for God's next move, they began working in the flesh, allowing Satan to have His way in their actions. I bet Satan had a blast, making the Chosen People of God commit spiritual adultery with a golden calf. The Enemy hates God's People with a supernatural hatred. We are created in God's image, and he knows that the only way he can knock us off God's path for our lives is to get our eyes off of the Lamb and onto ourselves. The Bible says that Satan comes only to "steal, kill and destroy," and when we leave the Sabbath Rest of Jesus and begin working in our flesh, Satan can have a field day creating chaos, busyness and confusion in our lives (John 10:10). Because we already have a natural tendency to walk in the flesh, we must choose daily to abide in the Sabbath of Christ, giving Him all our worries and cares and staying instep to what He's calling us to do each day.

Without the Sabbath of Jesus in our efforts, nothing we produce in this life will ever be pleasing to God. Our offerings will be like Cain's fruit of the ground—unacceptable. We must have the atonement of Jesus transforming everything we do. Job, another Old Testament man of faith, knew the impossibility of pleasing a perfect God. Even though Job was considered one of the most righteousness men to walk the earth (Ezekiel 14:14), he still couldn't give God a perfect 7. He knew that all he could offer God was his human 6, and he cried out for a mediator that could help him stand before God without His rod of judgment against him.

> *"He is not a mere mortal like me that I might answer him, that we might confront each other in court. If only there were* **someone to mediate between us***, someone to bring us together, someone to remove God's rod from me, so that his terror would frighten me no more. Then I would speak up without fear of him, but as it now stands with me, I cannot"* (Job 9:32-35 NIV).

We all need "someone to meditate" for us, and that is why Jesus is so important. God knew His Chosen People wouldn't be able to fulfill His holy standard (His law) without help, so He allowed them to run out of their efforts. God's Children had to come to a place where they knew without a shadow of a doubt that they couldn't produce a 7 on their own. When Jesus did finally enter the earth as the Answer to their lacking 6, the people were no longer waiting on the Lord. They were committing spiritual adultery, not with a golden calf this time, but instead with their multiplication of their 6's— with their own whitewashed efforts.

When the New Testament opens, John the Baptist begins to make bold claims about Jesus being the Messiah and about God's Spirit entering the earth. The prophet Malachi prophesied that the *"Sun of Righteousness will rise with healings in his **wings**."* I highlighted the word "wings," because in the Hebrew this word is *Kanaph*, which also means a corner of a garment. This garment is much like the large atoning blanket of the 7th day that covers the rest of creation. This is just another image in Scripture that reveals the atoning work of Jesus and His Sabbath Rest. Adam and Eve cover up their shame with fig leaves. Noah's sons cover his shame with a garment. Ruth who is in great need of a Kinsman Redeemer (symbolic of Jesus), asks Boaz to *"spread the corner of your garment over me, since you are a guardian-redeemer of our family"* (Ruth 3:9 NIV).

All of these coverings were made by the hands of people, but they can only cover our nakedness or shame in the natural. In order to cover the nakedness or shame before the eyes of a Holy God in the supernatural, the covering must be made by His hands. Two times we see God's hands sacrifice life, spilling Blood to atone for another life—in the Garden of Eden and on the Cross of Calvary. The first Blood spilled represents the Old Wine Covenant of the Law, the second represents the New Wine Covenant of Grace.

At the last supper, Jesus says something very interesting. He says, *"Take this and divide it among yourselves; for I say to you, I will not **drink of the fruit of the vine** until the kingdom* *of God comes" (Luke 22:17-18 NIV).* Notice that Jesus does not say wine. He says purposely the *fruit of the earth*, specifically fruit attached to a vine. Jesus' work on the earth, His efforts in the 6 of our world, was complete. The only thing left for Him to do was offer His body as a Living Sacrifice, so His redeeming salvation found in the Blood of the Lamb could pour out. And once His sacrifice was made, God's Kingdom would be established in the natural world; and through the outpour of the Holy Spirit, the Living Water, would rain down on the fruits of the earth, and produce the fruit rooted in The Vine of the Lord.

> *"For I will pour water on him who is thirsty, And floods on the dry ground; I will pour My Spirit on your descendants, And My blessing on your offspring; They will spring up among the grass Like willows by the watercourses" (Isaiah 44:3-4 NKJV).*

Jesus gave His disciples the New Wine (symbolizing His Blood) at the Last Supper and said that He would not drink of it again until the Kingdom of God comes. The second sacrifice committed by God's hand would be Jesus Christ, the Son of God, reconciling the earth to God's Kingdom once more. And through Jesus' Finished Work on the Cross, the Kingdom of God infiltrates the earth, represented by the presence of the Holy Spirit. But let's focus on the wine for a minute because what happens next confuses a lot of people. Jesus says that He will not drink of the fruit of the vine until God's Kingdom comes—after His sacrifice on the Cross, atoning creation and allowing the Holy Spirit to enter our world. However, as we read the crucifix story, we discover that He does drink wine. We will find that this is not an oversight because Jesus purposefully does something to show us what His Finished Work has accomplished.

Two times on the Cross, Jesus was offered vinegar, which is old wine that has soured. The first wine that He was offered was vinegar mixed with gall: *"And they went out to a place called Golgotha (which means 'Place of the Skull'). The soldiers gave Jesus wine mixed with bitter gall, but when he had tasted it, he refused to drink it" (Matthew 27:33-34 NLT)*. This gall, also called wormwood, can be found many times in different forms in the Old Testament. It gives the meaning of bitterness, especially in relationship to turning away from the Lord: *"so that there may not be among you man or woman or family or tribe, **whose heart turns away today from the Lord our God**, to go and serve the gods of these nations, and that there may not be among you a **root bearing bitterness or wormwood**" (Deuteronomy 29:18 NKJV)*.

There are several reasons Jesus did not drink the first vinegar (old wine) that was offered to

Him. First, Jesus' heart never turned away from God; He was obedient even unto death on the Cross. Therefore, He would not drink the vinegar with the gall because He held no bitterness in Him towards the Father. Second, the name "Wormwood" is a star that is unleashed after the 7th seal is opened in Revelation, which makes a third of the earth's water bitter. Jesus could possibly have not drunk the vinegar with the gall because His time of judgment would not occur until His second coming. Jesus' first coming was not to condemn the world but to save it: *"For God did not send his Son into the world to condemn the world, but to save the world through him" (John 3:17 NIV).*

Third, Jesus did not accept the first drink of old wine because several very important events happened between the two offerings: His garments were divided (Matthew 27:35), the sign stating that Jesus was *"KING OF THE JEWS"* was placed over His head (Matthew 27:37), He told one of His disciples to take care of His mother (John 19:25-27) and He even offered salvation to a criminal next to Him on the Cross (Luke 23:43). So Jesus waited to receive the symbolic wine until these events transpired. But I believe the most powerful reason that Jesus held out until the second offering of old wine was that He had to wait until the 6th hour.

Remember the number 6 represents the efforts of humankind. At the 6th hour the entire earth was covered in darkness. This darkness represents the shame that covered the earth because of the sin that we allow on the earth with our free will choices. And for 3 solid hours the sun went black, but suddenly the veil in the temple was torn (signifying that sin no longer separated God from His Children).

> *"Now it was about the **sixth hour**, and there was darkness over all the earth until the **ninth hour**. Then the sun was darkened, and the veil of the temple was torn in two. And when Jesus had cried out with a loud voice, He said, "Father, 'into Your hands I commit My spirit."' Having said this, He breathed His last" (Luke 23:44-46 NKJV).*

If the number 6 represents humans and the number three represents the Trinity, we can gather that Jesus waited until the 9th hour so that man and God could finally be reconciled through the Cross. With one arm Jesus grabbed tightly to a broken creation and with the other He held onto obedience to the Father; and through His broken body, His Blood poured out and all the earth finally found its Sabbath Rest. People were finally alleviated from trying to reconcile themselves to God in their own fruitless efforts. After the 9th hour, Jesus cried, *"I thirst!" (John 19:28).*

Now the time came for Him to drink the Old Wine Covenant of the Law, so He could give us the New Wine Covenant of Grace. Jesus consumed our failed efforts of achieving the Law, so we may live in the freedom of His grace. The fact remains that Jesus never drank the symbolic New Wine of His Blood; rather, He drank the Old Wine, so He could make a statement that He had fulfilled the law and freed us from our self-efforts to justify ourselves before God. And today we are so blessed to live in a time that Amos prophesied about.

> *"Behold, the days are coming," says the Lord, "When the plowman shall overtake the reaper, And the treader of grapes him who sows seed; The mountains shall drip with sweet wine, And all the hills shall flow with it" (Amos 9:13 NKJV).*

Can you imagine it? We live in a time that the New Wine (His Blood) is literally dripping from the mountaintops and flowing down the hills. Our world that has been corrupted by sin is now overflowing with the atoning Blood of Christ. The word *Sabbath* literally means atonement in Hebrew. Therefore, we are living in a time of God's holy and awesome atonement of our world that was separated from Him because of sin. Jesus Christ has fixed all wrongs and reconciled us back to God. He is Lord over Sabbath! God the Creator is resting on the Sabbath because He knew that the Slain Lamb of

Christ would finish His work through His sacrifice at the 9th hour on the Cross.

How awesome that we live in God's Rest and Jesus' Finished Work. Just before His death, Jesus cried out on the Cross: *"When he had received the drink, Jesus said, 'It is finished.' With that, he bowed his head and gave up his spirit"* *(John 19:30 NIV).* Jesus gave up His Spirit on this earth, so we can be filled with the Holy Spirit. He died, breaking His body, so His Blood could atone the whole world. We can have Jesus' Finished Work living abundantly in us if we press into His presence and wait on His timing.

> *"In the Cross is salvation; in the Cross is life; in the Cross is protection against our enemies; in the Cross is infusion of heavenly sweetness; in the Cross is strength of mind; in the Cross is joy of spirit; in the Cross is excellence of virtue; in the Cross is perfection of holiness. There is no salvation of soul, nor hope of eternal life, save in the Cross." — Thomas à Kempis*

Personal Application

1. How does your life demonstrate every day the joy you have because of the New Wine of Grace that Jesus Christ died to give you?

2. No matter the troubles the day brings, how does knowing that you have been reconciled back to the Father through the Finished Work of Jesus Christ provide you with a peace that the world cannot offer?

3. How does knowing that Jesus is able and ready to redeem the brokenness and emptiness of your life with the power of the Cross erase the pain and guilt you may carry?

The Finished Work of Jesus on the Cross is more powerful than your worse sin. Your shame is nothing compared to the love and grace God has for you through His Son. Today, you can claim peace and joy because Jesus has rescued you from an eternity separated from God. You no longer have to live with guilt, fear or doubt because Jesus carried them to the grave and left them there.

"God, I will no longer allow my life to be filled with feelings that are not part of Jesus. Through the Finished Work of Jesus on the Cross, I have every right to claim victory over feelings of doubt, fear, hopelessness and depression. I claim the Blood of Jesus over my life, over my family and over my situation. I choose to rest in Your Sabbath Rest, so I no longer have to feel inadequate and alone. I pray this in Jesus' name, amen."

Chapter 6

The Vineyards

"Whatever you do, work at it with all your heart, as working for the Lord, not for human masters, since you know that you will receive an inheritance from the Lord as a reward. It is the Lord Christ you are serving" (Colossians 3:23-24 NIV).

The first mention of a vineyard is right after the flood. Remember how important the first mention of something is in the Bible? God is introducing a theme in the Bible that will run its course throughout the rest of Scripture. This theme will be a part of the wine analogy, and it's rooted literally in the fruits of our efforts on earth. Consequently, Noah's story also starts with the first rain in Genesis chapter 7 verse 4: *"Seven days from now I will send rain on the earth for forty days and forty nights, and I will wipe from the face of the earth every living creature I have made"* (NIV).

However, the first mention of rain actually occurs much early in Genesis chapter 2 verse 5-6, right after the 7th day of Sabbath when God rested from His creation work. The verses read, *"Now no shrub had yet appeared on the earth and no plant had yet sprung up,* **for the Lord God had not sent rain on the earth** *and there was no one to work the ground, but streams came up from the earth and watered the whole surface of the ground"* (NIV).

This verse obviously has physical significance, but it also has great spiritual meaning. Jesus, the Living Water, had not yet been sent to the earth. The fall of people hadn't happened yet, and Adam and Eve were still freely able to walk with the Lord. However, only one chapter later Adam and Eve use their free will to experience sin for the first time. Now the earth and Adam's human efforts are cursed: *"...the ground is cursed because of you. All your life you will struggle to scratch a living from it" (Genesis 3:17 NLT).* That's why the career choice of Adam and Eve's sons, Abel and his brother, Cain, is so important. Abel chose shepherding, relying on the sacrifice of the lamb instead of struggling to rely on his own self-efforts.

Cain in Genesis chapter 4 cultivated the ground after God said that the earth wasn't ready yet. Obviously, the ground would eventually be ready, and today the crop of the ground holds a beautiful image of God's abundance: *"The land yields its harvest; God, our God, blesses us" (Psalm 67:6 NIV).* Yet, before the rains had fallen, the harvest was not pleasing to God. Instead of waiting on God's time and relying on God's provision, Cain decided to establish his own crops and make the earth bend to his command. God needed to send His rain first before the crops would grow in His blessing. Jesus is compared to Living Water, so God wanted His people to hold off working the ground until He sent the rains down from heaven, alluding to our need for the supernatural flow of Jesus in our work.

But Cain didn't wait. He took his eyes off heaven, circumventing God's will, and focused on the dirt. He dug deep to find springs of water from the earth. He sidestepped God's plan, producing crops that provided security in his own effort instead of relying on God. Cain's act of disobedience influences the people of the world, causing almost all of them to walk away from the Lord. They were so busy establishing themselves that they didn't spend the precious time with the Lord during the "rainless years," learning to walk in step with Him and lean on the sacrifice of the lamb.

Cain went his own way, producing counterfeit crops that were not pleasing at all to God (Genesis 4:6). And because He did not wait, all the earth's people went astray: *"The Lord saw how great the wickedness of the human race had become on the earth, and that every inclination of the thoughts of the human heart was only evil all the time" (Genesis 6:5 NIV).* Sin had entered the earth, and God had purposely given His people a barren wilderness, forcing them to rely on Him. However, instead of depending on God for their provision like Abel, they established their crops in their own efforts.

Finally, the rains did come, and God filled the corrupted lands with a flood of His holiness, sweeping away anything not rooted to Him. God had purposely created a drought after the fall of man, so earth's people could learn to depend on Him—yet they ignored the wilderness and created crops, so they perished in His waters. Waiting and relying on God prevent us from walking away from God during the delicate time that we are maturing in Christ and growing in faith.

It's important to keep in mind, though, that God purposely gave us free will on the 6th day, knowing that we would make choices that would separate us from our Holy God. That is why God created His Sabbath Rest on the 7th day. He knew that Jesus, Lord over the Sabbath, would die to forgive the fruit we create in disobedience and to redeem the fruit we create in obedience. The whole point to creation and redemption is that God wants us to create fruit on this earth for Him that will live on into eternity. God created us in His image and He is a Creator. We waste our talents when we bury them in the dirt, and we mock the sacrifice of Jesus who died to redeem our efforts. That is why the vineyard theme is so important.

The first thing Noah does after he finally leaves the ark is he plants a vineyard. God had made him a "man of soil" knowing that he would be the first to plant a crop after God had sent His rains.

> "Noah, a man of the soil, proceeded to plant a vineyard. When he drank some of its wine, he became drunk and lay uncovered inside his tent. Ham, the father of Canaan, saw his father naked and told his two brothers outside. But Shem and Japheth took a garment and laid it across their shoulders; then they walked in backward and covered their father's naked body. Their faces were turned the other way so that would not see their father naked" (Genesis 9:20-23 NIV).

Since this is the first mention of a vineyard, it is also the first mention of drunkenness. We don't know if Noah purposefully drank to excess or if his wine fermentation experiments to preserve the grapes went a little awry. Nevertheless, something had definitely changed on earth that Noah had no prior experience with. The fruits of the earth now were filled with rain from heaven—the Living Water—instead of simply the water from the ground. The water represents God's holiness and, therefore, His judgment of anything that is not holy. And since Jesus has not yet broken His body on the Cross and poured out His Blood of salvation to the earth, this water exposes the shame of all who fall short of God's glory, including Noah.

> *"Therefore no one will be declared righteous in God's sight by the works of the law; rather, through the law we become conscious of our sin" (Romans 3:20 NIV).*

Nakedness symbolizes our shame, and our self-efforts will always lead to our shame without the salvation of the Cross. We can never produce anything worthy of God without the redeeming work of Jesus. God Himself says that the human heart is inclined to sin: *"...every inclination of the human heart is evil from childhood..." (Genesis 8:21 NIV).* Noah's nakedness is similar to the nakedness in the Garden of Eden that Adam and Eve experienced.

The Bible is showing us that even though humankind received a second chance, we are still living in a world separated from God. We still need coverings of grace for our nakedness and shame. Two of Noah's sons use a handmade garment to cover their father's nakedness (much like the fig leaves sewn together by Adam and Eve), and his two sons make special care not to look at Noah. However, the third son stares onto his father's nakedness.

God is using this situation to share valuable insight with us. First, God is setting up a theme of the vineyards and exposing that our efforts are still not good enough without the supernatural work of a Savior redeeming them. God's holiness still stands, but we do have the promise that God gives us second chances. We can't boast in our works because without salvation, they mean nothing. We can only boast in the Lord. That is why God loves a humble spirit. Our humility allows us to joyfully expect grace, so our lives can be pleasing to God. The only way to do this is to take our eyes off our nakedness, and fix them unwaveringly to the Cross. Our Sabbath Rest comes from knowing that it is all about Jesus' Finished Work on the Cross and not about us. Praise God we live in a time of grace—a time that all the prophets dreamed about.

> "Therefore, as it is written: 'Let the one who boasts boast in the Lord'" (1 Corinthians 1:31 NIV).

Second, God is giving a warning to all of His Children. When Ham looked on his father's nakedness, he was standing in a position of judgment. Ham was using his eyes to judge Noah's shame instead of covering him with the grace of a garment. Therefore, Ham received a curse that he will always be the lowest, and his lineage (the people of Canaan) would live out this curse for the rest of their lives. Canaan means "lowland" in Hebrew. The truth of the matter is that every person on earth has shame. We all make mistakes and none of us will ever be perfect in the natural, so we have no right to stare at the nakedness of others and stand in a position of judgment over them. That is why God is very big on mercy. Jesus said in His famous beatitudes: *"Blessed are the merciful, for they will be shown mercy" (Matthew 5:7 NIV).*

For this reason, Canaan (descendants of Ham) was cursed, but his brothers, Shem and Japheth, were blessed. As Christians, we will be exposed to the shame of others. It doesn't mean we ignore it. Shem and Japheth didn't ignore their father's nakedness. However, they did take great care not to stand in judgment of their father. We will all be Noah at one point or another. We will all find ourselves naked before judging eyes or we will be a part of watching someone's nakedness. This is not the time to stand in judgment. God exposes the sin of people He loves, so they may become more like Christ. And it is our job to offer a garment of grace, so we may receive the same blessing as Shem and Japheth.

The New Testament also mentions vineyards, specifically in Jesus' parables. One of His parables is about a Vineyard Owner Who leases

His vineyard to farmers. The only problem is that the farmers will never offer the fruits of their crop to the Owner. The Owner begins to send His servants to the vineyard, reminding the farmers to produce a crop for Him, but the farmers mistreat all the servants and send them away empty-handed. Finally, the Owner sends His Son, but the farmers killed Him, thinking that somehow they could have the vineyard for themselves. However, the Owner destroys the deceitful farmers and gives the vineyard to others who will offer the fruits to the Owner. Many parallels can be made from this parable, but I want to focus on the work of the farmers.

> *"He had one left to send, a son, whom he loved. He sent him last of all, saying, 'They will respect my son.' But the tenants said to one another, 'This is the heir. Come, let's kill him, and the inheritance will be ours.' So they took him and killed him, and threw him out of the vineyard" (Mark 12:6-8 NIV).*

The vineyard represents our work on this earth, and God expects our fruit to be offered to Him. What we can glean from this story is that we are cultivating a crop that does not belong to us—we are only tenants. God owns everything, and we have the privilege of being part of His Kingdom and His Master Plan on this earth. However, our efforts must be aligned with God's heart or else we are just throwing Jesus out of our vineyards. We were created to make beautiful offerings that glorify God. Although we will never be perfect, we can be faithful to serving God and working the land He has given us. We must not be tempted to offer fruits according to our flesh, like Cain. His fruit might have looked good, but God knew it wasn't rooted in the vine of obedience; rather, it was rooted in his self-preservation.

It's easy to trick ourselves into thinking that our hard work will be pleasing to God because, at least, we are not burying our efforts in the dirt, like the man from The Parable of the Talents. This man had a distorted view of God because he lacked a true relationship with Him. Instead of using his talents in good stewardship to the Lord, he buried them with excuses based on ignorance and lies. The man condemned the Master of being a hard man Who was a cheat. His view of our all-loving God full of goodness, mercy and truth is so far from reality that it's absurd and even outrageous to those of us who have an intimate relationship with God.

> *"Then the man who had received one bag of gold came. 'Master,' he said, 'I knew that you are a hard man, harvesting where you have not sown and gathering where you have not scattered seed. So I was afraid and went out and hid your gold in the ground. See, here is what belongs to you'" (Matthew 25:24-25 NIV).*

However, we merely are spinning our wheels, allowing ourselves to be seduced by a counterfeit crop when it's not rooted in the Vine of Christ. It doesn't matter how busy we look if our work is not done in obedience to the Holy Spirit, the Bible states that we are producing nothing of eternal value. Instead of the skewed view of the man who buried the talent, this attitude parallels the defiance of Cain—he worked to produce a counterfeit crop for the Lord, but none of his offerings were pleasing and he didn't understand why. Our work must be connected to the Vine of Christ if we want our vineyard to produce much fruit in eternity. *"I am the vine; you are the branches. If you remain in me and I in you, you will bear much fruit; apart from me you can do nothing"* (John 15:5 NIV).

Finally, when I read about vineyards, I'm also reminded of another very important person in the Bible who bought a field and planted a vineyard: The Proverbs 31 Woman. *"She considers a field and buys it; out of her earnings she plants a vineyard. She sets about her work vigorously; her arms are strong for her tasks"* (Proverbs 31:16-17 NIV). Women are in no way discounted from working a vineyard for the Father. If we were, I definitely wouldn't be sitting here writing this book. Writing takes too much time and it is a very lonely process. If my efforts were not rooted in the Vine of Christ, I surely wouldn't waste all my time, clicking away at this keyboard. But that is truly the important point. If our work is not done in obedience to the Holy Spirit, we are literally wasting away our efforts, energy, time and lives. It is not worth it. That's why we must always keep our eyes on Jesus, so the works of our hands and the fruits of our vineyards are done in obedience to His will. We must always work the True Vine, not the vine of our self-efforts.

> *"You have forgotten God your Savior; you have not remembered the Rock, your fortress. Therefore, though you set out the finest plants and plant imported vines, though on the day you set them out, you make them grow, and on the morning when you plant them, you bring them to bud, yet the harvest will be as nothing in the day of disease and incurable pain" (Isaiah 17:10-11 NIV).*

Yes, we need to work heartily unto the Lord: *"Whatever you do, work at it with all your heart, as working for the Lord, not for human masters" (Colossians 3:23 NIV).* We can't expect God to rain His blessings on a seed that we haven't planted. However, as we work, we should be fully aware that our efforts will never be pleasing without the Finished Work of Jesus. So we can give God our efforts, setting them at the foot of His throne, and wait patiently on the Finished Work of the Cross. Otherwise, we waste all of our days and energy worrying about details that don't matter unless we learn to give them to God and wait in His Sabbath Rest.

"More effort is exerted in planning and arranging than in waiting upon the Lord."
– Watchman Nee

Personal Application

1. Have you ever cultivated a promise of God when it wasn't time yet? What was the result?

2. Was there a time in your life when you stood in a position of judgment over someone instead of offering a covering of grace? Did you feel remorse afterward?

3. Have you planted faith-seeds for God to rain down His blessings upon? Are you waiting patiently for His rain or are you getting sidetracked by other counterfeit crops?

Don't get seduced to create counterfeit crops that glorify you instead of the Lord. Satan wants to keep you busy, producing things that are not eternally minded. Waiting on God is part of the process. Waiting shows that you trust that God will do what He says. Waiting makes you reliant on God for everything. Waiting is a necessity to your walk of faith and should not be overlooked as trivial.

"God, help me to wait and rest in the Sabbath Rest of Jesus Christ. I don't want to produce a counterfeit crop that doesn't glorify You. I want my work to transcend this earth to my eternal life with You in heaven. I desire the fullness of all the blessings You want to rain down on my life. Help me to keep planting those seeds of faith, and tell me when it is time to rest in the Finished Work of Jesus Christ. I pray this in Jesus' name, amen."

Chapter 7

Wine of Our Promise

"For we are God's handiwork, created in Christ Jesus to do good works, which God prepared in advance for us to do" (Ephesians 2:10 NIV).

When we receive a God-planted promise in our spirits, we literally become giddy with the intoxicating beauty and wonderment of the Father and His revelation. I remember when God poured out His revelation on me after His promise that I would write a book. It is God's initial outpour of wine that we bring with us on our journey through the wilderness toward our Promised Land. I was able to do so much with this first wine because I had so much joy thinking about and anticipating His promises coming to fruition. I fasted for over forty days within a one-year time span (drinking only water). I fasted meat, TV, alcohol, coffee, candy—anything that seemed fast-able, I fasted. I spent hours every day with the Lord. I read the Bible over and over again. Every restriction that

God placed on me, I embraced and fought for victory. I was obedient to every command God required of me because I drank from the first wine of His promises. I wanted to do everything in my power to achieve His promises and be worthy of receiving His blessings.

But I didn't realize that this first wine, much like the wine at the wedding, would run out. I continued to seek the Lord and write on my blog during my wilderness years. I read many books written by Christian influencers because I needed to encourage myself in the Lord. God pulled me out of public ministry, so I could focus on my personal ministry with Him alone. I served my family faithfully, and spent much of my time being a great mom and wife (which I still do). I had already written my debut novel when my first-born was a one-year-old; and by the time my third born was a toddler, God still had not fulfilled His promise to publish it, and my wine of giddy anticipation ran dry.

I didn't understand why it was taking Him so long to move supernaturally in my situation, and my previous anticipation and joy was wearing off with every year of drought that came and went. I kept trying to do everything in my power—humble myself, grow in wisdom, strengthen my faith—to force God's hand to move on my behalf, but nothing I did in my strength worked. I was left with the unmistakable truth that I had done everything in my power (given God all of my 6), but it still was not enough. I needed Him to give me His supernatural 7.

> *"Truly I tell you, if anyone says to this mountain, 'Go, throw yourself into the sea,' and does not doubt in their heart but believes that what they say will happen, it will be done for them" (Mark 11:23 NIV).*

I would tell that mountain standing between my promises and me to move, but it only seemed to get bigger and bigger with each passing year. I pushed at the mountain, tried to go over it, tried to go under it, tried to go around it; but nothing I did would get it out of my way. Finally, after years of trying, I learned to stay in step with the Holy Spirit and let Him deal with the mountain. I never realized that God was enlarging the valley (my personal ministry to the Lord) before He gave me my mountain (my public ministry to the Lord). We are called to serve God in both the public and private areas of our lives; however, many people focus too much on the public ministry—I know I did. But our private ministry is the foundation of our public ministry.

A large mountain of promise cannot fit in our Promised Land if we only have a tiny valley in which to place it. Often, God will take us out of public ministry for a time, so He can enlarge our valley and teach us the importance of it. If we never get the fact that our private ministry is paramount to a successful public ministry unto the Lord, we may neglect it and encounter serious problems. God will shake the foundation of our lives and anything done in self-glory and not for His glory will crumble. We must ensure that everything is sheltered in the valley of our personal ministry to the Lord.

> *"I shook out the folds of my robe and said, 'If you fail to keep your promise, may God shake you like this from your homes and from your property!' The whole assembly responded, 'Amen,' and they praised the Lord. And the people did as they had promised" (Nehemiah 5:13 NLT).*

We too will receive God's Mountain Promise. Our faith will explode with the initial wine, and we will begin our journey, leaving the bondage of selfishness and forging straight into the wilderness. We tend to think that our promises will come easily, and we may not realize how long the process takes. Or we may focus too much on the mountain, and neglect the valley. Our society today is accustomed to getting everything quickly, and we all want to do something awesome in our lives. But the insights we learn that really change us are absorbed over the long haul. Total transformation takes time, and we must be willing to commit to the process.

We want God to move fast and achieve His promises for us quickly, but that isn't the point. God cares more about our character and who we are becoming than He does about the things we achieve for Him. Obviously, as we are faithful to walk according to His will, we will produce great fruit for His kingdom. But if God were not so concerned about the process of refining us into the image of His Son, He would just take us home to heaven as soon as we receive salvation. There has to be a purpose for our struggle and pain on this earth for God to allow it.

> *"Consider it pure joy, my brothers and sisters, whenever you face trials of many kinds, because you know that the testing of your faith produces perseverance. Let perseverance finish its work so that you may **be mature and complete**, not lacking anything" (James 1:2-4 NIV).*

I like to tell my kids that this life is like a womb. God has tucked us into the belly of the natural world, which is encased in God's eternal spiritual realm. God wants us to grow and stretch and mature before we die because we are becoming the people we will be for eternity. We get many second chances in this life, but we only get one life to become who we want to be in heaven. The trials and struggles mature us, grow us, stretch us and transform us. Much like a bodybuilder pushes against the resistance of the weights to grow physically stronger, God allows resistance in our lives so we can grow spiritually stronger. The bodybuilder knows that she has only one chance to get into her best shape before the day of her unveiling. This is the same with us: whatever spiritual shape we achieve on this earth will follow us into heaven (Matthew 18:18).

> *"Let us not be surprised when we have to face difficulties. When the wind blows hard on a tree, the roots stretch and grow the stronger, let it be so with us. Let us not be weaklings, yielding to every wind that blows, but strong in spirit to resist."* – Amy Carmichael

Personal Application

1. Have you ever faced a mountain that separated you from the promises that God has given you?

2. What made you finally surrender to God's timing in your life? How does surrendering to God's plan encourage you to never give up?

3. Has God come through on a promise that He has given you or are you still waiting for Him to move that mountain?

God wants to move the mountain that separates you from your dreams, but He must allow the fulfillment of all that He has planned to come to pass first. It may seem like God is taking forever, but in actuality, His movements are perfect and right. You can learn to rest in Him, working and resting in accordance with the will of His Spirit. Continue to believe even when everything around you is telling you to give up.

"Father, I claim today that I know You will move that mountain that separates me from my dream.

I may not know when or how, but I believe the promises that You have given me will come true. I will not let doubt or the natural circumstances of my life dictate my belief. I will confidently wait on You, trusting that You can produce a miracle in my situation. I pray this in Jesus' name, amen."

Chapter 8

Lord Over Sabbath

"For somewhere he has spoken about the seventh day in these words: 'On the seventh day God rested from all his works'" (Hebrews 4:4 NIV).

The number 7 is similar to the number 3 because they both hold the meaning of completion. However, 7 is different because it can only be found after the number 6, and it carries with it the sense of fulfillment. The 7 is the fulfillment of the 6. On each day of creation, God created everything perfect and good—even the 6th day when he created humans. *"God saw all that he had made, and it was very good. And there was evening, and there was morning—the sixth day" (Genesis 1:31 NIV).* Nothing God created was fallen, corrupted or evil. However, God gave humans free will. We were made in the image of God, and God is a Creator. Therefore, God gives us free will to create a beautiful harvest that glorifies Him. The only problem is that free will can also be used to create things that bring no glory to Him. Things created in the presence of God (in obedience to Him) bring honor. Things created in the absence of God (in disobedience to Him) bring no honor.

Free will is first demonstrated in the Garden of Eden. One tree was the Tree of Life and the other tree was the Tree of Knowledge of Good and Evil, and these trees together establish our free will choice. Just like the Children of God entering the Promised Land, Adam and Eve had the free will to choose blessings or curses. The mere presence of two trees gave them a choice; thus, extending them the gift of free will.

> *"The LORD God made all kinds of trees grow out of the ground—trees that were pleasing to the eye and good for food. In the middle of the garden were the tree of life and the tree of the knowledge of good and evil" (Genesis 2:9 NIV).*

Once they ate from the Tree of Knowledge of Good and Evil, God had to sacrifice the first animal to cover up their shame, so He could stay in relationship with them: *"The Lord God made garments of skin for Adam and his wife and clothed them" (Genesis 3:21 NIV).* Could this be why God created the animals and humans on the same day: one would have to be sacrificed to restore the other, until the Great Sacrifice? God knew humans would sin using their free will, but He doesn't give up on the beauty we create for His glory because of the ugliness we create.

Moms and dads don't give up on their children just because they make mistakes. There is still beauty in a creation that has fallen. God knew we would fall into sin and corrupt His perfect world when He created us, which is why He made the 7th day—because Jesus would become our atonement, Sabbath Rest, fixing all our wrongs. He would redeem our efforts of 6, so that our offerings to God—no matter how shabby they look—would be pleasing through the Blood of the Lamb.

> *"Therefore, since the promise of entering his rest still stands, let us be careful that none of you be found to have fallen short of it. For we also have had the good news proclaimed to us, just as they did; but the message they heard was of no value to them, because they did not share the faith of those who obeyed. Now we who have believed enter that rest..." (Hebrews 4:1-3 NIV).*

Jesus said, *"The Sabbath was made for man, not man for the Sabbath. So the Son of Man is Lord even of the Sabbath" (Mark 2:27-28 NIV).* The Sabbath was created for men and women because God knew that we would fall short of His perfect standard. That is why He told us to rest on the 7th day because He knew that there was nothing more we could do in our own efforts. Jesus had to become "Lord over the Sabbath," so that creation could be brought back to the Holy Standard of God. Our work and efforts of 6 are redeemed in Sabbath Rest. It is interesting that the Bible warns us in Hebrews that *"since the promise of entering his rest still stands, let us be careful that none of you be found to have fallen short of it" (Hebrews 4:11 NIV)*. We know we will fall short of God's glory, but we don't have to fall short of His Rest. It is in the rest that God supernaturally transforms our works into pleasing offerings to Him through the sacrifice of Jesus—Who is our Sabbath Rest.

> *"For everyone has sinned;* **we all fall short** *of God's glorious standard" (Romans 3:23 NLT).*

There is so much power in our final rest to achieving our dreams. We offer God our 6 jars of effort that we have gathered through the years, trying to reach our promises in our own strength. We must remember that our promises are seeded in the spirit (because God is spirit), and there is no way they will manifest in the natural world without supernatural help. God allows us to work our 6 days for Him, and then He wants us to rest. Our 6 will never be good enough, but God knows that, and He's already written the solution into His master plan. He would send Himself into His creation, and redeem all our efforts on the 7th day by the sacrifice of the Lamb. Finally, we have the mediatory to Whom Job cried out for: *"If only there were a mediator between us, someone who could bring us together" (Job 9:33 NLT)*. That is why Sabbath is so important: we must always remember that Jesus redeemed the earth, making it holy once more.

> "Observe the Sabbath day by keeping it holy, as the LORD your God has commanded you" *(Deuteronomy 5:12 NIV)*.

The Apostle Paul was the authority on Sabbath Rest, and He discusses it in detail in Hebrews chapter 4. I would encourage everyone to read his profound words found in those verses. Paul understood that when we enter God's rest, we also rest from our own work. He also goes onto to warn us that when we don't enter into God's rest, we may fall into disobedience. This disobedience occurs when we rely on our own strength instead of resting in the Finished Work of the Cross. Some people assume that when Paul wrote about our rest in Hebrews, that he was only referring to heaven. But Paul explains that the Lord has appointed "today" as the day to enter this rest—not some distant future (Hebrews 4:7).

Does that mean Paul didn't believe in working unto the Lord? Not at all! In fact, Paul may have done more for the spreading of the Gospel than any other disciple. However, Paul understood that there were limits to his strength. He maintains that he purposely highlighted his weaknesses, so that Christ's power could rest on him. Paul chose to no longer strive in his human efforts. Instead, he made a decision to do as Jesus commanded and pick the lowest seat. It is only in this low seat that God is able to shine the fullness of His power in our lives through grace. And when we finally sit in the lowest place, we will enter into the rest of God—allowing the Finished Work of Jesus Christ to transform our 6 into His mighty 7.

> *"But he said to me, 'My grace is sufficient for you, for my power is made perfect in weakness.' Therefore I will boast all the more gladly about my weaknesses, so that Christ's power may rest on me"* (2 Corinthians 12:9 NIV).

Paul was a highly educated Pharisee (Acts 23:6). Paul also was a Roman citizen (Acts 22:25). This combination for a Jewish man would have made Paul an asset to the religious leaders of his time and skyrocketed his life into worldly acclaim and success. He was not a fisherman, tax collector or a zealot like the other disciples. Paul was a well-educated religious leader who ravaged the church and scattered believers before his conversion (Acts 8:1-3). Writing nearly half of the New Testament, Paul would be the last person to confess that he had weaknesses in the art of oration and discourse, yet that is exactly what he claims.

> *"And so it was with me, brothers and sisters. When I came to you, I did not come with eloquence or human wisdom as I proclaimed to you the testimony about God. For I resolved* to know nothing while I was with you except Jesus Christ and him crucified. I came to you in weakness with great fear and trembling" *(1 Corinthians 2:1-3 NIV).*

Paul of all people said that he would "resolve to know nothing." He didn't want to use his human eloquence and wisdom that he gained during his life of accomplishment. Paul knew that his human striving would never be pleasing to the Lord. No matter what, our efforts will always fall short of God's holy standard. Paul writes that we *"all are naked and exposed to the eyes of him to who we must give account" (Hebrews 4:13 ESV).* Just like Noah, we all have shame—no matter how educated, well versed and smart we think we are, God's holy standard will always judge us as unworthy. But thankfully there is an answer. Because of God's great love for us, He sacrificed His only Son, so that He could become our High Priest on this earth and the Great mediator between a sinful world and a holy God.

We can give up our human striving, finding rest in the lowest seat, so Christ's atoning work on the Cross can transform our human efforts into a powerful force of God. Paul understood that his best would never compare to God's perfection, so he entered into Sabbath Rest, allowing the ministry of Jesus Christ to take full reign. Maybe the reason why Paul had such an influential ministry in this world was that he learned to enter into God's Rest. Not only was his work pleasing to the Lord, it also had supernatural power that transcended this earth into eternity. Therefore, Sabbath Rest makes our lives peaceful, pleasing and powerful forces of God.

> *"My message and my preaching were not with wise and persuasive words, but with a demonstration of the Spirit's power, so that your faith might not rest on human wisdom, but on God's power" (1 Corinthians 2:4-5 NIV).*

Personal Application

1. How can you use your free will to produce something in this fallen world that not only glorifies God, but allows Him to establish His presence in your efforts?

2. Do you believe that today you are living in the Sabbath Rest of Jesus because of His finished Work on the Cross? How can you choose to enter into this rest every day?

3. How can you make Sabbath Rest not just a day of the week, but a total lifestyle change?

Sabbath Rest is not just a Sunday or Saturday, it is a way of believing that transforms the way you live. When you acknowledge and believe the power of Sabbath Rest, you will revolutionize your entire life. While the entire world is caught up in human striving, God will pour out His abundance on your obedient efforts of 6 and your resting in God's 7.

"God, I don't want to live like the world—never having enough, never being good enough, never

living eternally minded. I want to live according to Your best design and embrace the system of Sabbath Rest that You have established through Jesus Christ. Lead and teach me in Your rest. Help me to find victory in Jesus' Finished Work, so I can be an example to the world. I pray this in Jesus' name, amen."

Chapter 9

New Pentecost

*"And all were amazed and perplexed, saying to one another, 'What does this mean?' But others mocking said, 'They are filled with **new wine**'"* (Acts 2:12-13 ESV).

We know that the law given to Moses on Mount Sinai for the Old Testament on the first day of Pentecost held a high standard of holiness for people, but what we may not realize is that Jesus came with the highest standard of holiness—God's standard. The law states that we can't murder: *"You shall not murder" (Exodus 20:13 NIV)*, yet Jesus says to even hate someone in your heart is murder: *"You have heard that it was said to the people long ago, 'You shall not murder, and anyone who murders will be subject to judgment.' But I tell you that anyone who is angry with a brother or sister will be subject to judgment..." (Matthew 5:21-22 NIV)*. The law states that we can't commit adultery: *"You shall not commit adultery"(Exodus 20:14 NIV)*, but Jesus says that lust found in our hearts is adultery: *"You have heard that it was said, 'You shall not commit adultery.' But I tell you that anyone who looks at a woman lustfully has already committed adultery with her in his heart"* (Matthew 5:27-28 NIV).

What God gave Moses on Mount Sinai were laws that focused on the outer performance of people, but the law couldn't discern the human heart. And try and try as they may, God's People could only keep an impression of His holy standard for a time, but what's in the heart finally comes out, and they would either forget the laws or corrupt the laws to suit their own desires. Jesus said Himself, *"But the things that come out of a person's mouth come from the heart, and these defile them. For out of the heart come evil thoughts—murder, adultery, sexual immorality, theft, false testimony, slander"* (Matthew 15:18-19 NIV).

Jesus enters the world, giving us new laws that hold us to the highest standard, and the laws are not directed at our actions; they are directed to our hearts! But there is no way we can possibly attain Jesus' highest standard when the Prophet Jeremiah says that *"The heart deceitful above all things and beyond cure..."* (Jeremiah 17:9 NIV). With what we know about the human heart, attaining God's perfect standard is impossible. However, Jesus would not give us a command that we could not keep. The good news is that Jesus gave us God's highest standard of holiness, knowing that in our 6 we could never fulfill it, because He would fulfill it for us in His 7. Jesus gave us the law and sacrificed Himself on the Cross, so that our effort of 6 could be supernaturally transformed to God's holy standard by Jesus' offering of 7—our atonement. We didn't earn this, but it is a part of the beautiful gift of Sabbath Rest. We rest on what Jesus has accomplished for us.

Peter discovered another profound truth concerning the number 7. Peter asked Jesus, *"Lord, how many times shall I forgive my brother or sister who sins against me? Up to seven times?"* Jesus answered, *"I tell you, not seven times, but seventy-seven times" (Matthew 18:21-22 NIV).* The multiplied 7's are emphatically stressed here. They are so beautiful after we discover how they transform our efforts of 6. What we discover from this verse is that Jesus not only gives us grace so our best (and remember our best is considered filthy rags) can be pleasing to God, but He gives us grace so that our worst can be forgiven.

The most amazing thing occurred after Jesus' death and resurrection—we and all creation were finally reconciled back to the Father. God allowed free will on the 6th day, knowing that Jesus would finish His work on the 7th day. Christ accomplishes what Ezekiel foreshadows in the Old Testament: *"I will give you a new heart and put a new spirit in you; I will remove from you your heart of stone and give you a heart of flesh" (Ezekiel 36:26 NIV).* With our new hearts and with the forgiveness of the Cross our lives can be a holy offering to God. The works of our hands and the crops we create for God will be pleasing offerings in God's sight because of Jesus. And if we ever doubt the power of Jesus' Finished Work on the Cross, we only need to look at the New Testament Pentecost.

After the resurrection, Jesus told His disciples to wait: *"I am going to send you what my Father has promised; but stay in the city until you have been clothed with power from on high" (Luke 24:49 NIV).* The wait signified that Jesus is about to do something that only He can do. The disciples could do nothing in their 6 during this time of waiting, so they had to abide in the Sabbath Rest prepared for them. After they waited, they received the third part of the Holy Trinity: The Holy Spirit. The Holy Spirit could finally come into the lives of God's Children because His perfect standard had been met. Finally, God's holy requirements were fulfilled and Jesus took our punishment, so we could have the righteousness necessary to stand before a holy God.

> *"When the day of Pentecost arrived, they were all together in one place. And suddenly there came from heaven a sound like a mighty rushing wind, and it filled the entire house where they were sitting.*

And divided tongues as of fire appeared to them and rested on each one of them. And they were all filled with the Holy Spirit and began to speak in other tongues as the Spirit gave them utterance" (Acts 2:1-4 ESV).

When the New Pentecost arrived and Holy Spirit was released onto the world, the disciples were filled with God's power and authority. They began preaching and prophesying, and all the devout people in Jerusalem at the time could understand everything being said in their own language: *"And how is it that we hear, each of us in his own native language?" (Acts 2:8 ESV).* Peter stood up and preached to the gathered people and 3,000 souls were saved that day! It isn't a coincidence that some onlookers mocked the disciples and said that they were drunk on **New Wine**. *"But others mocking said, 'They are filled with **new wine**'" (Acts 2:13 ESV).* Indeed, they were drunk on the revelation and transformation of the New Wine of Christ's Blood poured out onto the earth! Jesus had consumed the Old Wine of Law and unleashed His New Wine of Grace. The Holy Spirit had finally arrived, and they were indeed drunk on the supernatural presence of God!

Once we realize that Jesus' spilled Blood of atonement is the New Wine, and His body is the bread that was broken on earth to bring forth the Wine, we will do whatever it takes to have an abundance of His Wine and Bread in our lives! We will give God everything He desires from us because we know that He wants to multiply the Supernatural Wine of Christ in our careers, ministries, families, relationships, finances, health, minds and hearts! We will hold nothing back from God, knowing that He is not trying to hurt us—He is trying to bless us!

> *"Honor the Lord with your capital and sufficiency [from righteous labors] and with the firstfruits of all your income; So shall your storage places be filled with **plenty**, and your vats shall be overflowing with **new wine**" (Proverbs 3:9-10 AMP).*

We can be confident of two things: our relationship with God has been reconciled through Christ and now God wants to bless us abundantly. The New Testament Pentecost is proof that Jesus' 7 has redeemed the entire earth! We can celebrate the Pentecost, knowing that God gave the laws and Jesus fulfilled them. We can go boldly to the throne with our prayers and requests because Jesus has made a covenant of redemption for His People with His Blood. The covenant is signed and binding, and all who have faith in the Finished Work of Jesus on the Cross receive righteousness by grace, so they may come to God even in their sinfulness, carrying great expectations of God's best.

Our self-righteousness will always fall short, so we are free to focus on the righteousness that

Jesus' Finished Work on the Cross has accomplished in us. When we keep our eyes on Jesus, we will want to please Him out of our great love for Him and our great gratitude for what He has done for us. We will be loved into doing God's best because of the grace of the Cross, not shamed into it because of the guilt of the law.

> *"So now there is no condemnation for those who belong to Christ Jesus. And because you belong to him, the power of the life-giving Spirit has freed you from the power of sin that leads to death. The law of Moses was unable to save us because of the weakness of our sinful nature. So God did what the law could not do. He sent his own Son in a body like the bodies we sinners have. And in that body God declared an end to sin's control over us by giving his Son as a sacrifice for our sins. He did this so that the just requirement of the law would be fully satisfied for us, who no longer follow our sinful nature but instead follow the Spirit"* (Romans 8:1-4 NLT).

Personal Application

1. How does knowing that Jesus will always redeem your efforts and complete your works done in obedience to the Holy Spirit encourage you to step out on faith for God?

2. How can you rest in your situation today "until you have been clothed with power from on high"? Why does waiting on God help you in the end?

3. Jesus didn't come to condemn you. He came to free you from your human inadequacies. Can you walk in this grace, allowing your obedient efforts to be made pleasing to God?

God's plan all along has been to give you both free will and Jesus, so applying them together you can live righteously on this earth, producing a crop that is pleasing to God. All the works you offer God that have been covered by the Blood of Jesus will remain with you in heaven for eternity. God did not leave you alone in your human shortcomings. He knew you would fall short, which is why He made His Son the center of His great plan. You don't have to live in fear of condemnation—you simply need to rest in the Finished Work of Jesus Christ on the Cross.

"Father, I want to live for You. I want my efforts to always be covered by the Blood of Jesus. Today, I offer You my work, my family, my efforts and my life—please cover it all with the redeeming Blood of Jesus. I want my life to be a pleasing aroma to You. I want my work to count for eternity. Don't let me waste one more day in human striving. I trust that You can accomplish amazing things in my life if I will only rest in Your Sabbath. I pray this in Jesus' name, amen."

Chapter 10

New Beginnings

"For I am about to do something new. See, I have already begun! Do you not see it? I will make a pathway through the wilderness. I will create rivers in the dry wasteland" (Isaiah 43:19 NLT).

Once Jesus produced the New Wine at the wedding feast in Cana for His first miracle, using His 7 after the hosts had given all the 6 they had in them, a New Beginning was created for the celebration. The importance of letting Jesus do His 7 while we rest, is momentously overlooked today. Even though we are a greatly blessed people, we are completely worn out with our efforts of 6. God Himself rested on the 7th day, knowing that Jesus was the embodiment of creation's complete fulfillment. That's why resting in the Sabbath Rest is so important. Yes, there is a literal Sabbath at the end of each week, which we are commanded to enjoy; but there is also a spiritual Sabbath that many people miss. Instead of resting on the 7 that Jesus sacrificed to give us, we work and work, trying to offer God our counterfeit 7 only to fall short.

All we can create in our own effort is a bunch of 6's, and any more than one 6 becomes an unacceptable offering to the God—in fact, it becomes the antichrist spirit because we are no longer relying on Christ. Satan loves for us to dwell in this self-reliant state because he can eat away at our actions done in the flesh since we are not moving in the spirit. We must listen closely to what the Holy Spirit is telling us to do. We can always find ways to sacrifice, give, work and do more for God, but if we are not doing our efforts in obedience to God's will, we are working in the flesh and our offerings will not be pleasing to Him.

There is something wonderfully special about the number 8, especially since it follows the number 7. It means New Beginnings. God saved 8 people on the ark to establish a new covenant after the flood (Genesis 7:13). The 8th day, which occurs after the 7th (Sabbath), begins the new week of our work unto the Lord. God made a new covenant with Abram (changing his name to Abraham), which included the circumcision of every newborn male on his 8th day (Genesis 17:12). This covenant reaches past the natural into the supernatural, allowing all who enter into covenant relationship with Jesus Christ to have their sins cut away to become new creations. We have a new life in Christ.

"This means that anyone who belongs to Christ has become a new person. The old life is gone; a new life has begun!" (2 Corinthians 5:17 NLT).

The great thing about the 8th day is that we finally see a harvest produced from all our natural work of 6 after Jesus' supernatural work of 7. Jesus resurrects our efforts and pours out His abundance. We spend years and years planting a harvest by faith. We see very little evidence of our crop, but we know it is there. We must wait on the latter rains, so our natural work can be transformed by the supernatural finished Work of the Cross. King David knew what it was like to wait on God, but he continued to rely on God's faithfulness alone and not his own strength. He gave God his 6 and chose to stay in the Sabbath Rest, so the Lord could provide His saving 7.

> *"But as for me, my prayer is to you, O Lord. At an acceptable time, O God, in the abundance of your steadfast love answer me in your saving faithfulness" (Psalm 69:13 ESV).*

If we try to reap a harvest before Jesus' transforming power kicks in, we will have a crop that lacks His supernatural abundance. And we already know that our efforts are fruitless if they are not done in obedience to the

Holy Spirit and His Word, the Bible. Waiting is difficult because it takes faith. Christian thinkers and writers throughout time have discussed in detail the challenges that they faced trying to wait on the Lord.

Obediently waiting can be a painful discipline to master because we are giving God complete control of the situation, which causes us to put all our trust in Him. We may say that we trust God with our words, but our actions show that we don't trust Him at all! The best way we can show God that we believe in His promises and we trust that all things will come out according to His good plan is to wait. One of my pastors, Dave Cotham, always asks me, "How do you spell *FAITH*"? And the answer is constantly the same, "*WAIT.*" Waiting is one of the hardest steps of obedience Christians can take, but it truly reveals our faith!

For many years, I have written for God, planting obedient seeds into His Kingdom. I've seen some fruit of my efforts, but I'm holding out for God's fruit! I didn't work this long and hard, sacrificing 10's of thousands of hours in obedience to the Father to reap a pathetic harvest in my 6. I know what I can do in my strength alone, and it is minuscule. I want God's strength. I want His abundance. I want the harvest only He can produce with His glory in the Sabbath Rest of Jesus!

So I will wait until I know for certain that Jesus has completed my work of 6 with the power of His 7. I will stay in my Sabbath Rest, knowing that God will unleash His best when the time is right. Nothing less is worth it to me. I won't touch my crop of obedience until God says so. *"Let us not become weary in doing good, for at the proper time we will reap a harvest if we do not give up" (Galatians 6:9 NIV).*

When God finally releases us to reap a harvest, an awesome thing occurs: not only are we blessed, but God's Children everywhere are blessed. God loves all His Children, and He chooses to use each of us to fulfill the needs of the world. When God produces a great harvest in our lives, He will use that harvest to care and provide for His People. I truly believe that much of the world's needs would be met if Christ-followers would give God their efforts of 6 and rest in Jesus' 7. If we would just stop our striving and working in our own strength and abide in the gentle leading of the Holy Spirit every day, we could do so much more. But we have to trust the Father. Waiting for Jesus to supernaturally bless our crops may take a lot of waiting, but eventually, the waiting will pay off, and Jesus will multiply every crop done in obedience to Him.

> *"Now he who supplies seed to the sower and bread for food will also supply and increase your store of seed and will*

enlarge the harvest of your righteousness. You will be enriched in every way so that you can be generous on every occasion, and through us your generosity will result in thanksgiving to God" (2 Corinthians 9:10-11 NIV).

One of the most amazing promises found in Scripture for those of us who think we may have messed up our lives and crops too much for God to use is found in the Book of Joel.

"The Lord says, 'I will give you back what you lost to the swarming locusts, the hopping locusts, the stripping locusts, and the cutting locusts. It was I who sent this great destroying army against you'" (Joel 2:25 NLT).

The Lord sent devastation to God's Chosen People because they had forsaken Him. They disobeyed His commands and took control of their own destinies—without relying on their All-knowing God. Therefore, the consequences of their decisions were devastating. God had already warned them to choose blessings or curses: *"Today I have given you the choice between life and death, between blessings and curses..."* (Deuteronomy 30:19 NLT). However, once God's people repented, He was quick to redeem and restore them. But according to Joel 2:25, not only did God restore them, He gave them back everything they lost during the wasted years when their disobedience had devoured their abundance.

This is good news for us today. All of us have seasons in our lives where we know that we disobeyed God, and many of our years in relationship with Him were wasted in our self-occupied pride. However, the Lord says that if we humble ourselves and repent, He will restore everything we squandered. This means that no matter how much we messed up, we can always finish well. We can still gain our full reward from God; it is never too late for us. God has an infinite imagination and the world's resources at His disposal, so He can ALWAYS write a new Plan-A for our lives that still includes our fullest reward in Christ.

We must never conclude that our bad decisions will prevent God from having His will accomplished through us once we acknowledge our sin. When we repent and submit our lives to God, He is more than capable of restoring all that we have lost. No matter how much the locust of our disobedience have devastated our crops, the full harvest can supernaturally grow in the most desperate areas of our lives, if we would only turn to Jesus for His redeeming salvation.

> *"Therefore do not throw away your confidence, which has a great reward. For you have need of endurance, so that when*

you have done the will of God you may receive what is promised" (Hebrews 10:35-36 ESV).

Personal Application

1. Have you ever experienced a time of New Beginnings in your life? Did this new beginning follow a time of great need?

2. Is there an area of your life that you have been planting many faith seeds? Are you anticipating the day that God will send His rain?

3. Have you produced a bunch of 6's in an area that you always feel lack? Can you choose to place your efforts in the Sabbath Rest of Jesus today?

Once you give your efforts to God, not only will He bless your work, He will restore what you have lost from your human striving in the past. God wants to establish His glory in your life. He wants to bless You with all of His abundance. When you submit your efforts in Sabbath Rest, they are covered by the Blood of Jesus Christ. He will take your work and bless the world with your efforts. So surrender them today and wait on the power of God to be unleashed in your life.

"God, I want Your strength, not my weakness. I want Your abundance, not my lack. I want Your power, not my helplessness. I hand over all of my efforts to You today, submitting them to the redeeming Blood of Jesus. Touch the work of my hands and make my efforts grow in Your grace and truth. Saturate my seeds of faith with the Living Water of Christ, so my life can be a great force in Your Kingdom Plan. I want my work to mean something in eternity. I want to create a crop that glorifies You. I pray this in Jesus' name, amen."

Chapter 11

The Valleys

"The mountains rose, the valleys sank down to the place that you appointed for them" (Psalm 104:8 ESV).

The Bible gives a beautiful description of the spiritual path that we walk on during our lives on this earth before we reach heaven. I've physically been to the Valley of Baka in Israel, and I felt greatly honored to see with my natural eyes what I had experienced in my spirit.

"Blessed are those whose strength is in you, whose hearts are set on pilgrimage. As they pass through the Valley of Baka, they make it a place of springs; the autumn rains also cover it with pools. They go from strength to strength, till each appears before God in Zion" (Psalm 84:5-7 NIV).

These verses greatly helped my walk of faith because I had no clue of what God was doing in my life. I didn't know why He was withholding my promises for so many years. I didn't know that He was refining my character, transforming me into the image of Christ. I never realized that He was widening the valley of my personal ministry to Him, so He could securely plant my Mountain Promise (public ministry) on an unshakeable foundation. I didn't realize that the pilgrimage to attaining God's dreams for me would be filled with so many tears, but God was with me every step of the way. Every time I wanted to give up, He would renew my strength, giving me hope to make it one more day. All my days of hope filled the years, and I can now look back over the beautiful valley and say that it is one of the most precious sights that I have ever beheld. I got to know God intimately in that valley, and I learned to rely, wait and abide in Him.

Valley of Baka (Baca) literally means the Valley of Weeping. Before we start our journey, God gives us His revelation wine with our promises. In our ignorance, we may think that our journey to the mountain will be quick and easy. But this is not so. Our selfish will must die and our human nature must be broken and submitted to the Spirit of God, which responds to the will of God. This is a painful process because our pride hurts as it dies; but with every layer of flesh that is exposed and circumcised, God gives us His grace, peace and joy. And according to this verse about the Valley of Baka, God knows that we will be weeping. He knows that our journey towards inner holiness will be filled with our tears. That's why the Psalms says that God records our every tear.

> *"Record my misery; list my tears on your scroll—are they not in your record?" (Psalm 56:8 NIV).*

We learn to know our own weaknesses and strengths in the valley before attaining our promises, which enables us to stand strong in our Promised Land. During our stretch in the valley, it's not a person, circumstance or resource that will propel us into our Promised Land. We can't focus on the natural world and the situations occurring around us; rather, we focus inside of us on the good work that God is doing in the innermost recesses of our lives. God can change our situations in an instant, but He will not do so if He knows we are not ready. However, the word, *ready,* doesn't mean what we think it means. He has us in the valley for a reason, and we can't cut that time short without severely limiting our abilities in the Promised Land.

We will never have enough strength, goodness or holiness to bear the weight of God's promises. There will never be a time that we will be *ready* without the supernatural, finishing work of Jesus in our lives. It took me so long to understand that. All those years in the valley, I kept asking, "When will I be good enough to receive God's promises?" But it wasn't about my ability; it was about His ability. It wasn't about my strength; it was about His strength. It wasn't about my goodness; it was about His goodness. It wasn't about my holiness; it was about His holiness. I realized that even as I gave God my 6, my efforts would fall short. I would never deserve His promises. I needed the supernatural power and presence of God's 7.

> *"But you have come to* **Mount Zion**, *to the city of the living God, the heavenly Jerusalem. You have come to thousands upon thousands of angels in joyful assembly, to the church of the firstborn, whose names are written in heaven. You have come to God, the Judge of all, to the spirits of the righteous made perfect, to* **Jesus the mediator of a new covenant**, *and to the sprinkled blood that speaks a better word than the blood of Abel"* *(Hebrews 12:22-24 NIV).*

I became ready when I gave God every ounce of 6 that I had in me, knowing that it was inadequate to achieve God's promises. Then, I obediently waited in Sabbath Rest for God to pour out His New Wine in my life, and the waiting is one of the most difficult things that a Christian can suffer through. But when Jesus pours out His New Wine, there will be no mistaking it for the work of people because it will be supernatural. When the master of ceremonies at the wedding feast of Jesus' first miracle tasted the wine, he didn't know the miracle that had happened. But even in his ignorance, he realized that the wine he was drinking was the best. He exclaimed, *"Everyone brings out the choice wine first and then the cheaper wine after the guests have had too much to drink; but you have saved the best till now "* (John 2:10 NIV).

Jesus knew what He created was the best. He didn't need to taste test it, and He didn't bother asking the servants or bystanders to taste it. He had the wine brought straight to the man in charge, the person everyone was looking to for approval of the ceremony—the master of ceremonies. And that man proclaimed for all to hear that this new wine was better than anything that had been served throughout the entire ceremony. The years of human effort spent making wine could not surpass one single moment of Jesus' supernatural touch of 7.

God is so amazing and so thoughtful that He will allow our efforts to be transformed by the redeeming work of Jesus. God doesn't need our work. He is complete in and of Himself. But in His great love for us, He allows our unworthy efforts to be a part of His glorious plan. That is why Jesus had to come to this earth. He brought us His 7 in order for our 6 to be complete in Him. And it is only through Jesus Christ that we can be a part of the amazing and mysterious purposes of God. Jesus is the perfect completion of all God's promises in our lives. Only in Jesus will we ever earn God's "yes" for our promises. That is why we need to stop focusing on our efforts and start focusing on the Finished Work of Jesus on the Cross. Yes, we need to give God a crop to bless with His "yes," but we will know that the "yes" only comes from the shed Blood of the Lamb. He alone makes our offerings unto the Lord pleasing.

> *"For no matter how many promises God has made, they are 'Yes' in Christ. And so through him the 'Amen' is spoken by us to the glory of God (2 Corinthians 1:20 NIV).*

Although I was impatient for a time for God to fulfill His promises for my life, I did finally submit myself to obedience in the valley. God had important work for me in my valley before I could reach my mountaintop. What I never realized was that the Valley and the Mountaintop are one and the same. Together they make up the fullness of my ministry. The valley is how I minister to God in private—my husband, my family, my personal time with God—everything done in secret makes up my private ministry unto the Lord. My mountaintop is how I minister to God in public—my devotionals, my blog, my books, my speaking—everything done in the open makes up my public ministry to the Lord. People will find themselves in a lot of trouble if they neglect their private ministries and put all their focus on their public ministries. There is an issue of motives that needs to be checked. If we are only serving God in public, our intentions may be rooted in self-glory or people-pleasing.

The truth is that every spiritual leader needs a point of humility. Without humility, our pride can blind us and start our path to destruction: *"Pride goes before destruction, a haughty spirit before a fall" (Proverbs 16:18 NIV).* God is so good that He will provide us our valley so that our mountaintop doesn't cause us to fall. At any time, we can climb back down to the valley, and minister in secret. Before David was anointed king, he acted as a shepherd. Shepherding was literally a valley experience. The sheep lived in the valleys, so the shepherds had to leave the public world and wander by themselves, caring for sheep.

My valley story is very precious to me. I cared for my three little children, sacrificing all my desires for a public life to be there for them. I gave my children all of me, knowing that the tender moments of their young lives were so fleeting and special. I had the privilege of leading both my sons and my daughter to Christ. God has given me prophecies for each of my children. I know them inside and out. They are my joy, and I would sacrifice a million mountaintops to have the relationship that I have with them.

I had such a desire to share Jesus with people, and God sweetly told me to start with my family first. I learned to share my faith confidently with my family. I started praying for my kids out loud. I began reading Scripture and devotionals to my kids. I soaked up God's love and poured it onto my children each day. I learned to live out my Christianity in front of the audience of my family. Not everyone's story will be like mine, but all of us have a small circle of influence that is closest to us. God wants our foundation in Him to be strong before He builds a larger platform for us, and part of making that firm foundation is to share Christ with the people next to us.

The other part of my valley ministry is my personal relationship with the Lord. I love spending time with God in secret. I know that part of God's decision to withhold my mountaintop for a time was that I would learn to fall deeply in love with my private ministry with Him. God is the source of the abundance that I desire to share with others. If I'm not receiving His heart for ministry every day, I can't minister to others with the heart of God. Our private ministries must parallel our public ministries. When our pubic ministries become large and we don't have the firm infrastructure of a constant intimate relationship with God, the public ministry will eventually collapse. That's why the valley is so important—we will need both valley ministry and mountaintop ministry to serve God faithfully.

> *"The central significance of prayer is not in the things that happen as results, but in the deepening intimacy and unhurried communion with God at His central throne of control in order to discover a sense of God's need in order to call on God's help to meet that need." – E. M. Bounds*

Personal Application

1. God does not waste our waiting. How is God refining you and preparing you for the promises that He has for you?

2. Is there something more that God is wanting from you? Is there any area that He wants to strengthen while you are walking the Valley of Baka?

3. Is there an area in your life that keeps you humble? How does humility prevent us from walking in our pride?

God wants you to have a place of humility—a place where you serve, receiving no credit, payment or honor for your work. All spiritual leaders must have an area where they get dirty from service and receive no acclaim from onlookers. This point of humility is like a shield, preventing God's people from getting burned by human glory that they were not created to receive. Don't shun the hard, thankless work because it is that very work that protects you from your own pride.

"Father, help me to enjoy the valley experiences of my life. I want to love You in the highs and lows and in the running and waiting. I know very soon I will be with You in heaven, so I want You to refine me as much as possible while I'm on this earth. I want to become a strong faith person for You. Fill me with Your peace in my waiting. I know that not a single day is wasted when it's submitted to You. I pray this in Jesus' name, amen."

Chapter 12

The Wilderness

"Then Jesus, full of the Holy Spirit, returned from the Jordan River. He was led by the Spirit in the wilderness, where he was tempted by the devil for forty days. Jesus ate nothing all that time and became very hungry" (Luke 4:1-2 NLT).

We read a lot about wilderness in the Bible. Abraham and Sarah had to move to the wilderness and wait beyond physical impotence before their promised child was conceived. Joseph had to wait 11 years as a slave and 2 years in prison before God made Him the second most powerful man in the known world. King David had over a decade delay, running from King Saul in the desert that surrounded the Dead Sea. The People of God had to live in the wilderness, eating manna from heaven for 40 years before they entered their Promised Land. John the Baptist had to call out from the wilderness when it was his birthright to teach in the Temple. And Jesus had to go straight into the wilderness for 40 days after John baptized Him and God made known, *"You are my Son, whom I love; with you I am well pleased"* (Mark 1:11 NIV).

There is a transformation that occurs in the wilderness: it breaks our flesh, it brings us closer to God and it teaches us to wait on the Lord. By default, humans are naturally selfish, except for Jesus who chose to lead by example, allowing the will of His flesh to be tempted. Being the perfect Son of God, Jesus set a record-breaking time of only 40 days in the wilderness, which is impossible for those of us who are not perfect. We work, live and breathe in a naturally self-occupied state. Watch any 2-year-old, and the selfish indicators of human nature become apparent. It is for this reason that God has to bring us through the process of transforming us into the image of Jesus, as we learn to be controlled by the spirit, not the flesh.

> *"And we all, who with unveiled faces contemplate the Lord's glory, are being transformed into his image with ever-increasing glory, which comes from the Lord, who is the Spirit"* (2 Corinthians 3:18 NIV).

To be spirit-filled, spirit-controlled or spirit-led means to step outside of our me-centeredness and walk in complete surrender to the Lord. And without a doubt, this is not a natural tendency; it is a choice. If Abraham and John the Baptist had to spend time in the wilderness learning to be led by the spirit, we must all come to the conclusion that we too will be led to the wilderness for a time. And when I mean *a time*, I mean a long time. We already learned how easy it is for people to offer God their self-efforts, and God tests our faithfulness during those seasons that He makes us wait on His timing. We have no choice but to walk the wilderness if we want to be transformed into God's best image of us. Remember, the people we are becoming now will be the people we are for eternity. Easy, wide roads always lead to our immaturity in Christ. The difficult, narrow roads lead to our transformation in Christ.

Comparing the lives and actions of King Saul and King David teaches us the importance of the wilderness and why it is necessary to reaching our God-given dreams. We all have our "kingdom" that God has prepared for us. We all have our designated vineyard that we have dominion over. Both King Saul and King David were given the same promise: they were both kings of Israel. However, they each treated this promise very differently. The distinction that occurred in their leadership can be traced to their anointing. These two anointings would represent the different paths they would take to enter their Promised Land. One king took the easy road straight to his mountain promise, but the other king took the long road through the wilderness.

Both Saul and David were unexpectedly anointed king by the same prophet— Samuel. Saul was looking for his father's donkeys (1 Samuel 9:3) and David was tending his father's sheep (1 Samuel 16:11). Saul's family somehow lost their donkeys. Donkeys are highly intelligent animals that are very affectionate. In ancient times they were symbolic of wealth and were used by the rich for transportation. The fact that Saul had several donkeys suggests affluence. The carelessness of caring for the donkeys indicates a great lack of concern as their guardian. Donkeys are pretty laid-back animals that are easy to care for. They can last long periods of time without food or water. Usually, only a predator can make donkeys run, and Saul did not take adequate measures to ensure their protection. Saul looked through many territories to find them, but his inattentiveness caused him to wander.

David obviously cared for his father's sheep. Even when a famous prophet arrived at his home, he didn't leave them until his father summoned him. Shepherding was considered a lowly job performed away from the city in the valleys of the wilderness. Servants did the shepherding or many times the last-born son, like David. Sheep are extremely helpless animals. Some scholars have suggested that without human intervention, sheep would already be extinct. They have trouble finding food and water, and they lack any ability to protect themselves from predators. In ancient times sheep were allowed to roam pastureland, so the shepherd had to stay alert and attentive. The shepherd needed to gain the trust of the sheep, so they would closely follow him. Shepherding was also a solitary job that garnered no prestige or acclaim from society.

David and Saul were anointed with the same oil, which comes from the Hebrew word *shemen*. Oil is symbolic for God's Spirit or Holy Spirit. Saul (1 Samuel 11.6) and David (1 Samuel 16:13) each received God's Spirit. Although they received the same oil, the containers that held their oil were vastly different. Samuel put Saul's anointing oil into a flask, which comes from the Hebrew word *pak*. This flask was man-made, and many times created from a fine mineral called alabaster. Samuel was prepared to anoint a king because God told him the day before. Not only did he have a flask of oil ready, he had a dinner with thirty prestigious guests arranged, a seat of honor prepared and the choicest slice of meat waiting. Samuel made a grand show of anointing Saul.

On the other hand, God told Samuel to put David's anointing oil into a horn, which comes from the Hebrew word *qeren*. Samuel may have feared to anoint David because King Saul was still ruling, so God told Samuel to say that he was offering a sacrifice to God and anoint the new king in secret (1 Samuel 16:2-3). I think God chose the horn for two reasons: First, the horn would hide Samuel's intention of anointing David. Second, the horn is not man-made and **represents** power and strength. The container of the oil signifies the main difference between Saul's and David's kingship. Saul was the human desire for a king. He was a tall man born in prestige.

Shortly after Saul was anointed, he was made king before the nation. There was barely any lag time between events—he went straight to his mountain promise, bypassing the wilderness. Saul would not submit to the Holy Spirit to become a king after God's own heart. He lived out most of his kingship in the flesh and not in the Spirit. All throughout his life, he lived to please man, not God. Saul was a flask.

However, David was God's desire for a king. He was anointed in secret, but God would not fulfill his mountain promise for many years. He was in his teens when he was anointed, yet he didn't become king until he was thirty (2 Samuel 5:4). During the many years David hid in caves and commanded his growing army, God was able to transform David into a man after His own heart. David's sole desire was to be with God. He lived out most of his kingship in the Spirit. All throughout his life, he lived to please God, not man. David was a horn, and in his Psalms, he spoke about his love for the Lord.

> *"One thing I ask from the Lord, this only do I seek: that I may dwell in the house of the Lord all the days of my life, to gaze on the beauty of the Lord and to seek him in his temple" (Psalm 27:4 NIV).*

God needs our willingness if He is to transform us into people after His own heart. We must learn to put His desires above the desires of others and ourselves. He also needs time to change us from the inside out. He wants us to victoriously lead in our designated territories, but we need to be willing to submit to the process. God wants to make our "prestigious" man-made flasks into Horns of Salvation — the likeness of Christ. When Saul was declared king, he hid himself from the people (1 Samuel 10:22). When David was declared king and finally brought the Ark of the Lord back home, he danced before the people (2 Samuel 6:16).

God wants us to dance in the promises that He's given us, but we need to ensure that the Saul (symbolic for flesh-controlled) in all of us dies, so the David (symbolic for spirit-controlled) thrives. David could have taken the kingdom in his own strength many times; but if He had, his kingdom would have surely been planted in the flesh and not the spirit. He would have produced counterfeit crops that would not please God. If David would not have obediently waited on God's timing—allowing his branches to be connected to the True Vine, his kingdom might not have had the honor of producing a special crop for Christ, producing the New Wine for the world. Jesus Christ would be born out of King David's royal lineage. That is why the wilderness is so important. If God has great promises for us, we must be prepared for the long haul through our personal wilderness.

Once we leave our wilderness and God plants us in our Promised Land, we must take care not to allow pride to build up in our lives, which is what happened to Israel after God established them in their Promised Land. Slowly but surely God's Children began to take their eyes off of God, and eventually they totally forgot about Him. It got so bad that they no longer blushed when they committed sins against the Lord: *"Were they ashamed when they committed abomination? No, they were not at all ashamed; they did not know how to blush..." (Jeremiah 8:12 ESV).* This is why God loves the wilderness, and why we must all walk through it. We are learning how to be completely reliant on the Lord.

> *"I cared for you in the wilderness, in the land of burning heat. When I fed them, they were satisfied; when they were satisfied, they became proud; then they forgot me" (Hosea 13:5-6 NIV).*

When our hearts are solely filled with God's love for us, it won't matter the blessings that come our way—we will always stay true to God because He has become the center of our lives. All the other benefits of God's glory (health, family, wealth, influence, etc.) are mere enhancers of the joy we already feel on a daily basis. God knows that true joy and peace are only found in Him, so He will not lead us into the temptation of forsaking Him. God will delay our promises until He knows they won't cause us to forget our source of life and love.

> *"Take courage. We walk in the wilderness today and in the Promised Land tomorrow."* – D.L. Moody

Personal Application

1. Why is the wilderness experience so important to God's plan? Have you walked the wilderness that leads to your God-ordained promises?

2. Have you ever imagined yourself dancing in your Promised Land? How can that image help encourage you to continue making your way through the wilderness?

3. Is God the center of your life? How can placing your focus on Him help you to live in joy everyday—no matter the circumstances in which you find yourself?

The wilderness experience will help you learn to always put God first. The wilderness exposes all of your intentions and strips you of all your human strengths. Knowing that the journey through the wilderness is part of God's ultimate plan will help you continue even when you want to give up. God is doing a good work in you that only the wilderness can produce. Thank God for the wilderness because only on the other side of it will you find your Promised Land.

"God, help me to enjoy the wilderness experience of my dreams. Even though my dreams seem distant and dead, I will believe You at Your Word. You gave me certain promises, and I trust that You will bring them to fruition. Help me not to harbor any bitterness toward You and Your plan even when it feels slow and delayed. I want to let go of my control and cling onto You. I pray this in Jesus' name, amen."

Chapter 13

The Miracle of Faith

"As they went away, Jesus began to speak to the crowds concerning John: 'What did you go out into the wilderness to see? A reed shaken by the wind?'" (Matthew 11:7 ESV).

It is interesting to note that the Bible never describes John the Baptist doing any miracles. He didn't cause a small jar of oil and flour to continually pour out (1 Kings 17:16), he didn't resurrect the dead (1 Kings 17:22) and he didn't call fire from the sky (2 Kings 1:10), which were all miracles that Elijah performed. Yet, Jesus said about John: *"...of all who have ever lived, none is greater than John the Baptist..." (Matthew 11:11 NLT)*. Wow! There must be something about John's faith that supersedes the manifestation of miracles. John's miracle can be found in Malachi's final words: *"See, I will send the prophet Elijah to you before that great and dreadful day of the Lord comes. He will turn the hearts of the parents to their children, and the hearts of the children to their parents; or else I will come and strike the land with total destruction" (Malachi 4:5-6 NIV).*

John did something that was probably more difficult than raising the dead: he had faith in God's promises during a complete spiritual drought, causing people to repent and their hearts to be ready for the coming Savior: *"And so John the Baptist appeared in the wilderness, preaching a baptism of repentance for the forgiveness of sins"* (Mark 1:4 NIV). John became a wellspring of faith that saturated the wilderness, producing a revival for the Lord. Because of John's witness, men and women understood that their efforts at serving the Lord with a pure heart were not sufficient. They would always fall short of God's holy standard without supernatural grace—they needed a savior. John prepared the hearts of the people for a Savior completely by faith!

Producing faith when all circumstances seem dead and impossible is extremely difficult, but it is a choice. When we base our promises on God's faithfulness alone, the situations and people around us won't deter our hope in God's promises. That's why God will take us out of the public realm into the wilderness, so we can base our faith steps solely on Him. Much like Peter walking on water, we must keep our eyes on Jesus and not get distracted by the crashing waves around us. If Jesus tells us to walk in a circumstance that appears impossible, we can be sure that He will provide us a supernatural 7 to do so if we don't doubt.

> *"'Come,' he said. Then Peter got down out of the boat, walked on the water and came toward Jesus. But when he saw the wind, he was afraid and, beginning to sink, cried out, 'Lord, save me!' Immediately Jesus reached out his hand and caught him. 'You of little faith,' he said, 'why did you doubt?'" (Matthew 14:29-31 NIV).*

Finally, the time of the Messiah had arrived, but all the religious people with their access to the Scriptures and prophecies of the Messiah completely missed what was right in front of them. It is curious that they missed it, but John the Baptist got it—there may be something very special about John making his home in the wilderness. Obviously, John had been in the wilderness for quite some time since he was dressed in camel clothes and well versed at catching locusts and finding honey. He left the public world of ministry to focus on his personal ministry unto the Lord. The Hebrew word for *ministry* is *sharath*, and it means *to serve*. With a Christian world so focused on leadership, it is a great reminder to us that we are called to serve. We serve God by serving His people in public ministry, but our public ministry must parallel a private ministry that we have with the Lord. Jesus had a very public ministry, but His disciples always noticed that He would slip away to be with God.

> *"Yet the news about him spread all the more, so that crowds of people came to hear him and to be healed of their sicknesses.* ***But Jesus often withdrew to lonely places and prayed****" (Luke 5:15-16 NIV).*

Even Jesus, the Son of God, had to slip away from His public life to spend time with God in secret. If the Son of God, Who is God in the flesh, needed to refresh His soul away from the public eye, we are no different. That is why our quiet time with the Lord is so important. Cultivating this time does not come naturally. I remember teaching each of my kids to read. When they first started reading, they would wiggle in their seats, they would become easily distracted and they exhausted themselves trying to focus on the letters. But as I sat with them, patiently coaxing them to continue, they got better and better at it. Their wiggling subsided, they could focus longer and they started making sense of the letters. They started to learn to read.

The same thing will happen during our quiet times. God knows that we are going to struggle at first. He knows that we will wiggle, lose our focus and have difficulty making sense of the Bible. But He sits patiently at our side because He enjoys being with us and He understands that we are still learning. If we keep coming to God even when we feel like we are not getting it, a miracle will happen—we will start to learn the things of God and create a deeper relationship with Him. So we don't have to give up even when we feel like a kid learning to read for the first time. God loves us, and He wants to spend time with us even when we wiggle.

So let's return to John in the wilderness. We will never know why John willingly chose to leave town and go into the wilderness. It may be that his aged parents died or he did not fit into the School for Levitical Priests or he felt God calling him. For certain, the wilderness is close to the Lord's heart and it is the landscape to which we all must enter. As a child, John's parents would have gone over the prophecies in the Scriptures with him because of Zacharias's tongue-tied experience with the Archangel Gabriel and Elizabeth's womb-hopping moment with Mary.

However, it was John's time in the wilderness that God was able to capture the prophet's full attention. Then God was able to give John the Baptist the faith he needed to proclaim the coming Messiah with such boldness that even the religious leaders left their busy establishments of pomp and self-glory to venture into the wilderness to see what all the ruckus was about. Maybe if the religious leaders had focused on their personal ministry as much as their public ministry, they would have been sensitive to the amazing days they were living in—the Messiah among them.

For Christians with a large public ministry, the theme of the wilderness is so important. We can get caught up with the things happening on the mountaintop of our ministry and neglect the valley. People can be demanding, and we see them with our natural eyes. God, however, is not demanding, and He patiently waits for us to spend time with Him. He dwells in the spiritual realm; so when we want to spend time with Him, it is best to get into the wilderness, away from the loud noise of the world. We sometimes think we don't have time to get alone with God, but the truth is that we waste time when we don't.

God will prepare us for our day. Through the revelation of the Holy Spirit in our lives, He will get us ready for our public ministry. God's ways are best, perfect, powerful and eternal; and when we don't seek His ways every morning, we will waste most of our day running around in our effort of 6 instead of resting in the Sabbath of Jesus' 7. Yes, we may eventually get to the conclusion that God intended, but we could have saved so much time, energy and resources if we would have gone to God first, allowing Him to align our strength with His.

We discussed Christians having large public ministries and small private ministries, but we can also learn much from Christians who have large private ministries and very small public ministries. They have a life filled with faith in God's goodness and His Truth, yet they rarely venture out into public to share and apply what God is teaching them. Once we fully experience the great joy and peace we have in our intimacy with the Father, it may be tempting to pitch a tent and stay in our private ministry forever. Peter was faced with the same temptation. Jesus took Peter, James and John high up the mountain because He was about to do a "private ministry" that would be seen through the eyes of only three disciples. However, one day the Transfiguration that happened on the mountain would be known to all Jesus' disciples in the world.

Remember the valley represents our personal ministry with the Lord, and the Mountain represents our public ministry to the Lord. Jesus was giving His three friends an intimate picture of His divinity, and Peter was so completely moved by it that He wanted to make the mountaintop his home for good.

> *"And Peter said to Jesus, 'Lord, it is good that we are here. If you wish, I will make three tents here, one for you and one for Moses and one for Elijah'" (Matthew 17:4 ESV).*

What if Peter had built the shelters and Jesus, Moses, Elijah, Peter, James and John had stayed up there for good? It's not a coincidence that there were 6 men on top of the mountain, including Jesus. But there was something essential missing—Jesus' body hadn't been broken yet, and His Blood hadn't been spilled onto the earth, creating the atoning Sabbath that all of creation was waiting for. Jesus still needed to offer the sacrifice of His 7, and Peter didn't realize how much his idea of "pitching a tent" would have affected the world.

Our valley experiences with God are too beautiful not to share. We must be sensitive to the Holy Spirit's leading. He wants us to minister to Him in private, but He also loves His lost children. There are people out there who need to see and hear our valley experiences. They may be spiritually hungry and ready to receive every word that we give them. We don't need a huge platform to share glimpses of Jesus' divinity that the Holy Spirit has shown us. We can share it with our family, our friends, people at work or even total strangers. We will never know how much our words will influence the hearts of others. We may rest in the valley with God for a time, but He will lead us out into the public to be a messenger of Good News.

> *"How beautiful on the mountains are the feet of the messenger who brings good news, the good news of peace and*

salvation, the news that the God of Israel reigns!" (Isaiah 52:7 NLT).

Personal Application

1. Have you ever had to cling onto faith even when it felt like you were experiencing a great "spiritual drought"?

2. How is your quiet time with the Lord? Are you able to take time to sit with Him even when you feel restless or distracted?

3. Which ministry to the Lord is more comfortable for you—private or public? How can you serve the Lord in both areas of your life?

Ministry means to "serve," and God wants you to serve Him in the private corners of your life and in the public halls of the world. As long as you are staying obedient to God each day, you don't have to worry about having one ministry that is larger or smaller than the other because God will nurture both ministries in and through you. What direction is God leading you today? Take one step of obedience and God will help you minister to Him and to His people.

"God, help me to have the faith of John the Baptist. Even if every situation around me seems dry and lifeless, I want to believe that You are always there, ready to saturate the situation with Your goodness and glory. I claim provision, I claim abundance and I claim life in the bleakest of circumstances because I know that Jesus' power is alive and available to me today. I pray this in Jesus' name, amen."

Chapter 14

A Start in Selfishness

"I said, 'Plant the good seeds of righteousness, and you will harvest a crop of love. Plow up the hard ground of your hearts, for now is the time to seek the LORD, that he may come and shower righteousness upon you'" (Hosea 10:12 NLT).

We start every relationship in our selfishness. We get married because we have feelings of love for someone, and he or she makes us happy. We have kids because they will make our family complete and add value to our lives. We start a new job because we want it to help us on our road to success. We even start a relationship with Jesus in our selfishness because before He changes us from within, we are still slaves to sin. It's not until we accept the sacrifice of the Lamb of God that we become alive in Christ and dead to sin, and we can start our journey of transforming into God's glorious design for us.

"Don't you realize that you become the slave of whatever you choose to obey? You can be a slave to sin, which leads to death, or you can choose to obey God, which leads to righteous living. Thank God! Once you were slaves of sin, but now you wholeheartedly obey this teaching we have given you. Now you are free from your slavery to sin, and you have become slaves to righteous living" (Romans 6:16-18 NLT).

Once we receive salvation through Christ, God does not want us to stay in a selfish state, which is why Jesus' Finished Work on the Cross is so important. Jesus condescended Himself to the level of humanity, so He could reach into our own personal hells to get us out and bring us into the family of God. There are many definitions of heaven and hell, but I believe the simplest terms are that hell is the absence of God and heaven is the presence of God.

Before we accept Jesus as our Lord and Savior by faith, we are dwelling fully in our 6 where there is an absence of the Holy Spirit in our lives. Our works on this earth will never be pleasing to Him because they are not made perfect by Jesus' 7. But how merciful and loving is our God that He would send His Son into a world that He created perfect, which we corrupted with our flesh-focused free will choices. Jesus left His glory, dying on the Cross, so He could wrap our 6 up in His death and then resurrect it in the grace of His 7, atoning creation and allowing us to be a part of heaven where God dwells.

> *"Who, being in very nature God, did not consider equality with God something to be used to his own advantage; rather, he made himself nothing by taking the very nature of a servant, being made in human likeness. And being found in appearance as a man, he humbled himself by becoming obedient to death—even death on a cross!" (Philippians 2:6-8 NIV).*

We all start out in bondage to our sin. Sin comes in all shapes and sizes, but the single sin which Jesus died for was that *"We all, like sheep, have gone astray,* **each of us has turned to his own way**; *and the Lord has laid on him the iniquity of us all" (Isaiah 53:6 NIV)*. The mere act of going our own way is the ultimate sin—and we all do it! The ugly ramifications—adultery, stealing, lying, etc.—are merely outcomes of an inward choice. God set before us two opposing directions—we could choose the path of blessings or the path of curses. However, we all start in selfishness, so we must walk a path through the wilderness in a season that breaks the will of flesh—our desire to go our own way—so we can learn to walk in the spirit.

"Those who belong to Christ Jesus have crucified the flesh with its passions and desires. Since we live by the Spirit, let us keep in step with the Spirit" (Galatians 5:24-25 NIV).

I don't mean, however, to give the flesh a bad rep. In actually, it's not a negative word. The flesh is our body, our efforts, our personalities, our hearts, etc. Jesus had both flesh and a spirit just like us, and He was perfect. There is nothing wrong with having flesh; in actuality, the flesh of our 6 is very necessary for Jesus to do His 7. Like I said earlier, 7 comes after 6, and Christians can't be lazy in their natural and expect God to be powerful in His supernatural. The problem with our 6 occurs when the flesh rules over the spirit. The flesh cannot respond to the Spirit of God. The flesh cannot unleash the promises of heaven. Fruit seeded in the flesh (no matter how pretty and religious they look) cannot reach into eternity. The flesh is and will always be limited to the natural world if it is in control. However, if the will of the flesh dies and the spirit is allowed to control, the spirit will respond to God and the flesh must follow suit.

The spirit can grab hold of heaven's promises and manifest them into the natural world. All the fruits seeded in the spirit will bear fruit in the natural world and reach into eternity. But we must learn to let go of the wants and desires of our flesh and the limited understanding of our minds and trust the movement of the Holy Spirit. We can only learn to let go when we allow God to cut away all the people, circumstances and things that we find security in, so we can learn to place all of our hope and faith in Him alone. That's why the wilderness is so dear to God's heart; it brings us closer to Him.

To be certain, our flesh-oriented selfishness can also look spiritual—much like the religious leaders of Jesus' time. People can pour their selfishness into a human-controlled spiritual experience, creating a self-focused spiritual substitute. To illustrate this occurrence, I like to use the example of thirst. Research shows that many people do not know how to read their body cues. We confuse thirst for hunger, so we eat though we're really thirsty. Since our thirst never gets satisfied, we continue eating, hoping to quiet our need. When we finally do recognize our thirst, we go for sugar and caffeine loaded beverages that actually dehydrate us even more. We down our coffee and sodas, which seem to help for the moment, but an hour later our bodies start sending us more need-signals.

We live out these crazy lives filled with unending needs and desires, but we never recognize the true Answer to our cravings — we need water! Our need for water is spiritual, as well. We are born with an innate desire for our God. He designed us with a craving for His Spirit. However, instead of filling our cups with Him, we fill our plates piled high with food of the world. We eat of pleasures, worries, money, relationships, materialism; and we are never satisfied. We have become fat, indulged, ever-hungry people, and our Spirits are withering away to nothing. However, the Enemy knows that many people will catch on to the fact that they are spiritually thirsty, so he cleverly creates *Empty Spirituality*.

There are many beautiful tasting forms of spirituality that have always existed in this world. People drink them down hoping to quench their spiritual needs, but they only become more spiritually dehydrated: *"Jesus answered her, 'If you knew the gift of God and who it is that asks you for a drink, you would have asked him and he would have given you living water'"* (John 4:10 NIV).

I've come across a lot of "enlightened" spiritual leaders, books and schools of thought, but they are completely void of Jesus Christ and His sacrifice on the Cross. The Enemy sows many seeds of tantalizing insights that twist and change the Word of God. Then he strategically glosses over Jesus and His sacrifice for our sins—humanity's only true Hope. And the sad truth is that droves of people are getting a big dose of spiritually, but it's coming from the wrong side of eternity.

"My people have committed two sins:

They have forsaken me, the spring of living water, and have dug their own cisterns, broken cisterns that cannot hold water" (Jeremiah 2:13 NIV).

We are unable to dwell with God in His realm until we have our sins covered by the Blood of Jesus. Jesus' sacrifice atones for our sins, and we take on His righteousness. God cannot connect with us otherwise because He is perfect, holy and pure. Jesus is the only way to reach God. Why would God compete with "alternate" ways to His throne? Jesus would not have had to die on the Cross if another salvation plan could have been achieved. Jesus is our Sabbath Rest, and He is the atonement of all of creation! Jesus boldly declared His presence on earth as the Living Water to the people of the world: *"...Anyone who is thirsty may come to me! Anyone who believes in me may come and drink! For the Scriptures declare, 'Rivers of **living water** will flow from his heart'"* (John 7:37-38 NLT). Finally, the earth is flooded with Living Water, and many people are ignoring the true source of life raining down on them!

Jesus is God in the flesh Who came down to this earth so that we could commune with a Holy God. People die for the cause of Jesus Christ because they know He is the world's Answer for our spiritual need. Jesus is the Living Water, and we must not accept spiritual substitutes. We do God's Children a horrible wrong when we skip over the Cross. Jesus and His Finished Work on the Cross should never be a side-note. It should always be the main idea of every ministry we do. Spirituality will not get people to the presence of God—only Jesus will.

> *"For the Lamb at the center of the throne will be their shepherd; 'he will lead them to springs of living water.' 'And God will wipe away every tear from their eyes'"* (Revelation 7:17 NIV).

One other bondage of sin that tries to prevent us from experiencing the fullness of what God has for us is the spirit of "good enough." I discovered this first hand with my blog, alisahopewagner.com. I poured a lot of energy into my blog, watching it grow and its influences become broader. However, I began to rely solely on my blog to fulfill my public ministry, and I didn't cultivate the other vineyards that God had planned for me.

With my blog, I got instant feedback, and I had the satisfaction of actually seeing my influence (though very small) penetrate the world. It wasn't until God allowed my blog to hit a dry season that I realized how much energy I poured into my blog writing—to the expense of my other writing for the Lord. My book writing was all done in private and done by faith. There was no feedback and my work garnished very little satisfaction. I could gladly write on my blog all day, but writing and editing my books took much more effort.

I finally realized that I was limiting God's abundance in my life because I was getting caught up in the praise of people. I was so concerned with getting comments on my blog that I was unable to see the value in the writing that I did in secret. I finally saw first-hand how much I desired instant gratification. Although I continued to faithfully write on my blog, I stopped allowing my self-worth to be wrapped up in it. I wrote out of obedience and didn't bother with how many comments and shares I received. This helped me to place a higher value on all the work God was having me do—regardless of who was reading it. Now my satisfaction is based on my obedience to God and His pleasure in my work. I know that when the time is right, God will use my writing for His glory.

> *"The greatest test of whether the holiness we profess to seek or to attain is truth and life will be whether it produces an increasing humility in us. In man, humility is the one thing needed to allow God's holiness to dwell in him and shine through him. The chief mark of counterfeit holiness is lack of humility. The holiest will be the humblest."* – Andrew Murray

Personal Application

1. Is there an area in your life where you have "turned your own way"? How can you submit that area back to God?

2. Have you worked half-heartily at something, expecting God to bless your lack of effort? How can you give God your best, so He can bless your work with His supernatural abundance?

3. For anything to have true eternal value in your life, Jesus has to be the center of it. This allows His Blood to cover your work, so it can become a pleasing offering to God. Is there an area of your life that does not have Jesus at the center? Can you ask God to make Jesus the center once and for all?

Your life can be filled with God's best instead of humanity's good enough. Instead of settling for the world's offerings, which can bedazzle you at first but then leave you flat, it is better to wait for what God has in store. God's ways don't always make sense, and He doesn't abide by an instant gratification mindset, but He is worth the wait because only He can achieve miracles in your life. Learn to trust God to achieve the promises that only He can attain.

"God, help me to work hard for You. I know You want to grow me and strengthen me and mold me into the image of Your Son, Jesus. I don't care if my life looks good to the world if I'm living a spiritually empty existence. I want my life and efforts to have eternal value in Your Kingdom. Lead me, so I don't turn away from You and do my own thing. I don't want to sabotage the amazing promises that You have in store for me. I want to claim the fullness of Your abundance in my life. Fill me with faith, so that I can rest securely in You. I pray this in Jesus' name, amen."

Chapter 15

Yoking our Lives

"Don't copy the behavior and customs of this world, but let God transform you into a new person by changing the way you think. Then you will learn to know God's will for you, which is good and pleasing and perfect" (Romans 12:2 NLT).

The wilderness time will look different for everyone, but we each will feel it when it arrives. God will speak His promises over us, and we will tell Him that the quickest way to our destiny is to move from point A to point B in the shortest amount of time. But God will smile and gently say, "No, not yet. Come with me into this desert place for the time, so I can feed you sustenance from the Bread of Life and break you of your self-focused will." We'll be so pumped up about the promises we received from the Lord that we may charge right into the wilderness full speed ahead without realizing that this journey will not be a sprint; it will be a long zig-zag path of wandering, so God can do a major overhaul in our life.

Or we may be tempted to circumvent the wilderness, but we'll wind up jumping from promise to promise, never reaching the Promised Land that's just on the other side of the seemingly never-ending desert. The wilderness is much like a tomb of sorts. We are cut off from the veins of the world that feed our counterfeit security, so we can grow a large, singular artery to the Lamb of God. Once our total dependence on the Father is sure, He will unleash us to do many amazing and great things for His Kingdom. However, we must be certain that we resist the temptation to create a counterfeit 7 in our own strength of 6. Sometimes the waiting gets too long, and we wind up like the Children of God who made a golden calf. But if we want God's promises in our lives, we are going to have to give up the idols that we create in our impatience. An idol is any treasure or "mammon" that replaces God's position as supreme Lord of our life.

> *"No one can serve two masters; for either he will hate the one and love the other, or else he will be loyal to the one and despise the other. You cannot serve God and mammon" (Matthew 6:24 NKJV).*

I know I personally struggled with wanting to create idols while I waited for God to move in my life. I didn't know they were idols at the time until God brought me to a verse that I knew well: *"Take my yoke upon you and learn from me, for I am gentle and humble in heart, and you will find rest for your souls. For my yoke is easy and my burden is light" (Matthew 11:29-30 NIV).* A yoke is designed to be worn by two oxen. Whenever a yoke of oxen in the Bible appears, the pair are counted as a single unit. So in this metaphor, Jesus explains that we have a choice to yoke ourselves to Him, and when we do, our burden will be light. However, if we choose not to yoke ourselves to Him, many people think the other part of the yoke stays empty—that we are somehow able to walk freely without any outside influences. But that is not true. We are either yoked to Jesus by allowing ourselves to be spirit-controlled or we are yoked to Satan by allowing ourselves to be flesh-controlled. There is no in-between.

> *"For the flesh desires what is contrary to the Spirit, and the Spirit what is contrary to the flesh. They are in conflict with each other, so that you are not to do whatever you want" (Galatians 5:17 NIV).*

Once I realized that my yoke needed to be tied to someone, I had a great fear of doing anything outside of the will of God. I know firsthand how much the Enemy hates me and how he only wants to *"steal and kill and destroy"* everything in my life (John 10:10 NIV). I also understood that seemingly "good" works, like Cain's offering to God, could appear pleasing to the outside world, yet be very displeasing to the Lord if done in disobedience. For this reason, I continued to minister to the Lord in my private life, so He could search me to see if I was harboring any idol-making tendencies. I was very upfront with all my feelings of impatience, disappointment and frustration, but He was always gentle and patient, willing me to continue to stand firm and be courageous: *"Be on your guard; stand firm in the faith; be courageous; be strong" (1 Corinthians 16:13 NIV).*

I want my work to be seeded in the spirit so through the work of Jesus Christ, I can create eternal fruit even in my imperfect state. Every morning, I can make a decision to walk in the spirit. Only then will I know that my work will be done in accordance with God's will. Plus, I want to give God all my 6, but wait in my Sabbath Rest for Jesus to do His 7. If I am going to spend time planting eternal seeds, I want them to be watered by Living Water. That's why yoking ourselves to Christ is so important. God gives each of us a vineyard on this earth to create crops that are pleasing to Him. Having the Son of God yoked to my side, bearing the burden of my work and supernaturally blessing my crop is too good to pass up. Every morning, I want to invite Jesus with me, knowing that He will lead me on the path to His best.

I had the honor of meeting a Christian leader whose yoke with the Lord was obviously strong. Although Calvin Miller has gone to be with Jesus in heaven, his books and sermons continue to influence the lives of others. I got to see him speak, and I was so in awe of everything he said. I quickly went up to him after the conference and poured out my admiration and praises. Although he was very gracious to me, I could tell that my words didn't affect him. I remember walking away feeling very dejected, but God told me to simply take the beautiful insights I learned from Pastor Calvin and pay them forward to someone who needs encouragement. I didn't realize later that Calvin Miller had discovered something that I needed to learn.

I was reading one of his books, and he explained that he was so full of how God viewed him that the opinions of others couldn't add or take away from God's opinion. We are definitely meant to love and honor people, but in truth, people will let us down. If we love them with grace and mercy, our love will not change based on their actions. Pastor Calvin was so in sync (yoked) with the Lord, that the opinions of others would not sway him off of his course.

When we are doing our public ministry for the Lord, we will be confronted with the praises and persecutions of people. We can't let either sidetrack us from the good work that God is doing in us. We can discern if the Holy Spirit is trying to teach us something through the words of others, but we must not get distracted. We can get too comfortable with the praise and relax too long to enjoy it. Or we can get too scared of the persecution and allow it to stop us altogether. Instead, we should be so full of how God sees us that we continue to walk in step with the plans He has for us.

The mountaintop of our public ministry is done before the world. Everyone can see us and analyze all that we say and do. It can be hard not to get caught up in the hype all around us. That is why I think the valley is so important. Once our time on the mountain is done, we need to quickly go back to the valley and allow God to fill us with His Truth again. He can clean off the dust from our feet that we have gathered from serving others, and He can pour out His healing and Sabbath Rest into our lives.

Being closely yoked to Jesus will help us know when to go up to the mountaintop and when to go down to the valley. Jesus will lead us safely back and forth into our private and public ministries, so we can continue to run the race of endurance without losing hope and giving up. Once we fill ourselves so completely with His amazing opinion of us, we can faithfully love the people that God has called us to serve, which includes the ones who love us and the ones who hate us.

"Those who fervently love God are intoxicated by His warmth and live out their addiction like moths drawn to a flame." – Calvin Miller

Personal Application

1. Has an idol tempted you away from God's presence? Although an idol may look good at first, how does it transform once you place it above God?

2. Have you ever created a counterfeit 7 in your life? Did the end result disappoint you or leave you feeling empty?

3. Have you ever been praised by someone only to be persecuted by him or her days later? How can you find your security and worth in God alone?

Jesus is the only One that deserves the throne position in your life. Once Jesus is the center, He will give you power, strength and grace in all the other areas of your life. When you submit to Jesus, He takes your life and multiplies your efforts to the world. You don't have to worry about living a life without meaning because God places great value in you and your work, and He wants to share your obedient efforts with others.

"Father, help me to trust Your methods. I know that when I lose myself in You, I will actually find my true self. You are the only One who can multiply my efforts with Your supernatural power. I love You, Lord, and I want You to move in my life. I don't want the shabby harvest of my own efforts. I want to be yoked to Jesus, so I can find rest from all my human striving and limitations. I pray this in Jesus' name, amen."

Chapter 16

The Dying

"Very truly I tell you, unless a kernel of wheat falls to the ground and dies, it remains only a single seed. But if it dies, it produces many seeds" (John 12:24 NIV).

Jesus allowed Lazarus to die before He resurrected him from the dead. Not only was Lazarus dead, but he had been buried in a tomb and for 4 days. When Jesus told the people to roll the stone away from his tomb, Martha feared that Lazarus's body would smell: *"...But, Lord," said Martha, the sister of the dead man, "by this time there is a bad odor, for he has been there four days" (John 11:39 NIV).* The interesting thing about the whole story is that before Lazarus died, Jesus had said that it would not end in death: *"...This sickness will not end in death. No, it is for God's glory so that God's Son may be glorified through it" (John 11:4 NIV).* But to most of us, if the body of Lazarus is starting to smell of decay because he has been dead 4 days, the ending is death.

The "dying" part of the process allows God to reveal His glory; therefore, our promises have to die in the natural, so they can be resurrected in the supernatural. We've discussed the wilderness of our dreams, but there is something that happens after the wilderness and right before the Promised Land—we have to walk through the Jordan River. The Jordan River literally separated Joshua and God's Chosen People from their Promised Land: *"The priests who carried the ark of the covenant of the Lord stopped in the middle of the **Jordan** and stood on dry ground, while all Israel passed by until the whole nation had completed the crossing on dry ground" (Joshua 3:7 NIV).* The name of the Jordan River means "descender," and it carries the meaning of God bringing down the strength of people. God has to bring down our limited strength, so He can manifest His unlimited strength in us!

The Jordan River is also where John the Baptist baptized people. The physical experience of baptism symbolically illustrates dying to self and being resurrected in a new life with Christ. Jesus was baptized by John, demonstrating that He too would experience death in the natural, so His supernatural power and glory could be unleashed on this earth: *"Then Jesus came from Galilee to the Jordan to be baptized by John" (Matthew 3:13 NIV).* Every seed that is planted must die, so that the plant can spring to life.

The same goes for our promises. They must die, so they can live in Christ's abundance. Jesus said that Lazarus's story would not end in death, and He was right. It ended in a natural death, but this death is always a precursor to a supernatural rebirth. This theme is seen throughout the Bible, and our lives will be no different. God needs to take down our strength and let our dreams die in the natural, so we can have God's strength to resurrect our dreams in the supernatural.

This experience does not need to hurt if we wait in the Sabbath Rest of Christ. However, sometimes as we wait, God allows our dreams to fester. The promises of God almost seem to smell bad to us because we have waited so long and they have been dead for a long time. But we can be encouraged. The deader our dreams and the more they smell with defeat, the more alive they will become in Christ and the more they will shine His glory of victory. So if God has given us a promise, never stop believing. Wait in God's Sabbath Rest and remember that God has a knack of bringing the dead back to life. We simply need to let God "tear down our strength," so He can make the impossible possible in His strength.

Another example of God bringing the dead back to life is the Dead Sea. I've been there myself, and nothing around this massive lake can grow because of its salt-laden waters. The atmosphere surrounding the lake creates a yellow haze, and the hot sun shimmers off the salt-dusted sand. An obvious void of life encircles the briny, thick water for miles. Not only is the Dead Sea one of the "deadest" places on earth, it is also the deepest at 1,300 feet below sea level.

The "dead" and the "deep" attributes of the Dead Sea really struck a chord with me on my trip to the Holy Land. Ezekiel chapter 47 describes a symbolic rebirth of the Dead Sea. The Living Water of Jesus flows from the Temple and brings life to everything it washes over, including the Dead Sea.

> *"Then he said to me, 'This river flows east through the desert into the valley of the Dead Sea. The waters of this stream will make the salty waters of the Dead Sea fresh and pure. There will be swarms of living things wherever the water of this river flows. Fish will abound in the Dead Sea, for its waters will become fresh. Life will flourish wherever this water flows'" (Ezekiel 47:8-9 NLT).*

The Dead Sea receives water from the "holy place" and suddenly the waters become clean and the fish and the fruit trees are numerous. Jesus specializes in bringing dead things back to life. I know he has done that in my own life. I was dead to the eternal things of God until I found Jesus.

I also have learned that God will purposely create an area of lack or "deadness" in each of our lives, especially in the area of the promises that He has given us. Abraham, David and Joseph all had great areas of lack and need in the places God has given them promises. By faith they clung onto the hope of their God-given promises, and God showed up in mighty and miraculous ways.

God must make the lack "deep," so when He brings life to what is dead, He can fill it up with an abundance of His Living Water. No wonder the Dead Sea is also the deepest place on earth. The larger cavity of deadness will demonstrate a greater display of God's glory. The emptier we are of our strength, abilities and resources, the more we can trust that God will provide His miraculous power and authority in our situations.

God purposely leads us into large areas of need so our obedience will bring us to a place of deep deadness, causing us to trust that God will fill the hollowness He has created with His abundance. We can cling onto His faithfulness and be sure that He will fulfill His promises even when they seem dead and buried. The deeper and the deader our promises seem means that God is about to do something supernatural in our lives if we don't lose hope and keep the faith.

> "Abraham did not doubt God's promise. His faith in God was strong, and he gave thanks to God. He was sure God was able to do what He had promised" (Romans 4:20-21 NLV).

There is also another beautiful symbol of the Dead Sea that applies to our work for the Lord too. Many people are scared to do work for the Lord because they know their efforts will always be unworthy. I used to be that person. My fear of messing up made me want to bury my talents in the sand. However, God allowed a season in my life where people who did not know the Lord surrounded me. I tried to relate to them and honor their strengths. I humbled myself and learned from their expertise. I would try to drop little nuggets of truth into our conversations, but I always felt clumsy. I tried to communicate the amazing attributes of God and illustrate my personal relationship with Him, but it seemed that my words would get muddied up in the desert sand.

There was a wellspring of pure Living Water in me, but once it poured out of my lips and life, I would have no control over its movement and pureness. I would watch as the Living Water that I poured out got tainted and misunderstood. As it traveled through the minds and lives of people who didn't recognize that it was the source of all life, I wondered if I wasn't communicating effectively and I disparaged the fact that I didn't feel like a worthy vessel for Christ.

I finally prayed about sharing my faith and asked God to help me understand why I felt so insecure. I told Him that I didn't feel like I was doing a good job. If I could express the beauty of the Living Water more effectively, others would see what I see and drink deeply from its healing properties; instead they mocked my words and refused to taste from the drink I offered them. I opened the Bible and God gave me Ezekiel 47. In these verses, Ezekiel is taken to the Temple, and he watches as water pours from its doors.

The water flows from the Temple through the desert and into the Dead Sea. I imagined as the pure water from the Temple gathers debris, sand and dirt along its path. When it finally gets to the Dead Sea, the water is probably undrinkable because of all the dirt (remember the dirt symbolizes our flesh-efforts and the natural world). The Dead Sea itself is already so ruined that it cannot provide an environment to sustain life. It appears that the Living Water has no hope. The purity that once existed has entered into the heart of the Dead Sea where life cannot exist. But a miracle happens. The water is healed.

"Then he said to me, These waters pour out toward the eastern region and go down into the Arabah (the Jordan Valley) and on into the Dead Sea. And when they shall enter into the sea [the sea of putrid waters], the waters shall be healed and made fresh" (Ezekiel 47:8 AMP).

God taught me something amazing. I am His temple, and His Living Water pours from me into the desert places of the world. Once the water flows from me, I have to trust that God is in control of its movements. Because of God's grace, He allows His Son, Jesus, to gather the sins of humanity, so He can reach into our dead hearts with His love. Once He is able to penetrate our deadness, a miracle occurs: we are healed.

"And wherever the double river shall go, every living creature which swarms shall live. And there shall be a very great number of fish, because these waters go there that [the waters of the sea] may be healed and made fresh; and everything shall live wherever the river goes" (Ezekiel 47:9 AMP).

The Living Water brings to life what was dead, and an environment for growth begins. Therefore, I can't worry about what happens when I speak truth, and I can't focus on the fact that I will never be perfect. I just need to continue to pour forth the Living Water living inside my temple and trust Jesus' atoning work in the Sabbath Rest. The supernatural power of Jesus Christ will transform my dirty water in an abundance of His New Wine. As long as I continue to share the Bread of Life with others, continuing to multiply Christ's broken body to the world, His Blood and His saving grace will pour out. I don't have to worry about the dirt of my human efforts because the Finished Work of Jesus redeems it. When my work is done, I can rest in the Lord's Sabbath, knowing that God will be pleased with my work through the sacrifice of the Lamb.

> *"He called you to salvation when we told you the Good News; now you can share in the glory of our Lord Jesus Christ" (2 Thessalonians 2:14 NLT).*

What happens if we finally give our all to God and our efforts still die? We show God our 6 jars of dirty water, but they are never transformed into His New Wine. We discussed earlier about giving God our best and Him doing the rest in Sabbath Rest, but God may choose to allow our work to end and our expectations will not be met. My twin sister, Christina, and I used to have a newsletter ministry. We worked really hard at making this ministry a work of excellence and influence. Contributing writers would send in their articles, and we gathered their precious words into a quarterly collection. We had amazing themes, writers and photos. Our audience was growing, and we were getting great feedback. However, it became apparent that the amount of work became a heavy burden on us both, and we were faced with the decision of letting the ministry go. We didn't want to, but the Holy Spirit was making His move known.

Finally, after doing just one more newsletter, we accepted the fact that the ministry needed to die. But not for one second do I believe that the efforts my sister and I spent in our ministry were done in vain. God used it to teach us and to shape us. We gained many friends and we got to encourage the lives of others. But when God was ready to move, we had to get up and go with Him. If we would have disobeyed God and kept trying to pour our human efforts without His approval, our beautiful ministry would have turned into a horrible idol. I know for certain that God has all the seeds we sowed into that ministry. They might not have flourished right then and there, but He will replant them in a new vineyard that will thrive. Nothing done in obedience is in vain.

God's movements can't be comprehended, and we don't know the outcome of His twists and turns in our lives. The Children of God experienced God's unpredictable movements a lot when they were in the wilderness. The Pillar of Fire led them by night and the Pillar of Cloud led them by day. Sometimes the Pillar would stay a short time, but sometimes it stayed a long time. But when the Pillar started to move, the People of God had to pack their things and leave. God will do the same thing in our lives. We like to plan way in advance, and when God gives us a turn in our path; we are tempted to plan the move out until its completion. But we don't know when God is going to stop or move. We don't know when God will tell us to begin something and end it. All we can do is stay in step with Him every day, so we can be sure that when He says, "move," we move.

> *"And the Lord went before them by day in a pillar of cloud to lead them along the way, and by night in a pillar of fire to give them light, that they might travel by day and by night. The pillar of cloud by day and the pillar of fire by night did not depart from before the people" (Exodus 13:21-22 ESV).*

I remember walking the downtown streets of a large city. There were beautiful shops and restaurants and just looking at the uniqueness of each one made for an interesting afternoon. One store, however, stopped me cold. It was a wonderful gift shop with a sign across the door that read, "After 32 years of business, we are closing." I walked inside and saw the two owners, organizing what was left on the shelves. I felt so sad for their loss, but I could sense a peace in their demeanor. I was reminded of John the Baptist's words as he realized that he had accomplished the vision that God gave him, *"He must become greater; I must become less" (John 3:30 NIV).* John knew the truth that we must all learn: We are merely given a tiny, valuable piece of God's greater, ultimate plan. Though our part in it may seem to die in the natural, it actually thrives into the supernatural because of God's grace. He loves us so much that He would allow our human efforts to shape His Heavenly Kingdom.

*"Men come and go; leaders, teachers, thinkers speak and work for a season, and then fall silent and impotent. He abides. They die, but He lives. They are lights kindled, and, therefore, sooner or later quenched; but **He is the true light from which they draw all their brightness**, and He shines for evermore."* – Alexander MacLaren

Personal Application

1. Have any of God's promises in your life felt like they died? Are you still believing in them or have you given up?

2. How can waiting in Sabbath Rest help you to endure the loss of your dreams? Do you believe that Jesus can resurrect your God-ordained promises?

3. Do you believe that God is creating a cavity in your life that He Himself wants to fill?

God many times will create an emptiness in your life, so that He can fill it with His presence and glory. It may be tempting to try to fill that void with worldly things, but it is better to wait in your emptiness, believing that God will soon come with His bounty. There is beauty in emptiness because God delights in pouring out His blessings into the chasm that You allowed Him to make in your life.

"God, I want You to fill me. Don't let me try to satisfy my longing with lesser things. This world

can only offer me temporary relief, but You supply me with Your divine presence, which contains everything that my soul thirsts for. I want You in my life. I want the overflowing presence of Jesus Christ flowing in my thoughts, words and actions. Nothing else will ever be good enough. You are all I want. I know that You can supernaturally resurrect every dead promise in my life. I pray this in Jesus' name, amen."

Chapter 17

The Water

"When the ground soaks up the falling rain and bears a good crop for the farmer, it has God's blessing. But if a field bears thorns and thistles, it is useless. The farmer will soon condemn that field and burn it" (Hebrews 6:7-8 NLT).

The Bible has many themes on the Promised Land. God plants our promises across the wilderness at the foot of Zion, the place where He dwells. When we start our journey to our dreams, we usually start in a flesh-centered atmosphere (our strength, our resources, our abilities, our plans, etc.) but as we wander with God, we eventually learn to walk in a spirit-centered atmosphere (His strength, His resources, His abilities, His Ultimate Plan, etc.). Since all our promises from God are "yes" in the spiritual realm with Christ, we must learn to be controlled by the spirit, so the promises can be brought into the natural realm through our obedience: *"For all the promises of God find their*

Yes in him. That is why it is through him that we utter our Amen to God for his glory" (2 Corinthians 1:20 ESV).

God gives us these promises because they draw us out of our selfishness and into a Christ-centered state, which is the only way we can accomplish God's glorious plan in our lives (Psalm 85:5-7). As we start our journey to achieving our God-given dreams, the Holy Spirit will pour out His Spirit with the "early rain." This rain breaks up the soil of our hearts and allows God's seeds of promise to germinate. We obediently plant the seeds, working first in our flesh and then embracing the work in the Spirit. As we wait for the fruit of our obedience to ripen, we know that the Holy Spirit will pour out the "latter rain."

> "Be glad, O children of Zion, and rejoice in the Lord your God, for he has given the early rain for your vindication; he has poured down for you abundant rain, the early and the latter rain, as before" (Joel 2:23 NLT).

This latter rain ripens our small, bitter fruit with the sweetness and the fullness of the Lord. Without God's Spirit raining down on our lives, our efforts could never bless others with the supernatural power of God that manifests in both this world and eternity. A Promised Land without the Living Water of the Holy Spirit is a wasteland of constant thirst and emptiness. That is why patience is so important. We must wait for the Latter rain of Christ in our fruit, so we can have the fullness of His supernatural power in our efforts.

> *"Dear brothers and sisters, be patient as you wait for the Lord's return. Consider the farmers who patiently wait for the rains in the fall and in the spring. They eagerly look for the valuable harvest to ripen" (James 5:7 NLT).*

Also, as we work in our efforts (our 6), we need to realize that God will not always call us to use every resource at our disposal. He likes to show off His glory, and He needs a great lack in order to redeem. Yes, we give all your 6, but it must be in obedience to the Holy Spirit's leading. There will be times that we can give more resources, give more time and give more energy, but we will compromise the Sabbath Rest God has created for us. Also, we may be trying to accomplish God's promises in our own strength. He is trying to bring down our strength in order to promote His supernatural strength in us. Look at the story of Gideon.

Gideon started in his own strength and responded to God's call to action: *"The Lord turned to him and said, 'Go in the strength you have and save Israel out of Midian's hand. Am I not sending you?'" (Judges 6:14 NIV).* God let

Gideon start in his own strength, but to have the supernatural victory of God, he would eventually have to pass through the Jordan River. *"Gideon and his three hundred men, exhausted yet keeping up the pursuit, came to the Jordan and crossed it" (Judges 8:4 NIV)*. Gideon and his men were tired and overwhelmed because God had stripped their army to almost nothing. God needed to take down the strength of His Children, so they wouldn't claim victory for themselves. God said to Gideon, *"You have too many men. I cannot deliver Midian into their hands, or Israel would boast against me, 'My own strength has saved me'" (Judges 7:2 NIV)*.

In fact, Gideon had 10's of thousands of fighting men at his disposal, but God told him not to use them, so Gideon kept only 300 men. Gideon would exert all his strength, allowing God to use him to win the fight. Sabbath Rest doesn't mean we won't have to engage in the battle. Just the opposite—it means that God is using us in a supernatural way. If Gideon would have not trusted God and held onto the thousands of men, he might have won the war, but his victory would be rooted in his flesh, not the Spirit. The fruits of his efforts may not have had an eternal impact. Anytime we take the reins from God and play it safe with our natural eyes, we have now slapped God's hands away. Like a waltz, God will only lead if we submit to His steps.

Just because God is about to use us mightily, doesn't mean we charge ahead of God without listening to His instruction. We can throw everything into our fight for God's promises—compromising our finances, our families, our careers and even our time with God—and be in complete disobedience to God. Don't forget that God not only has His promises for us, He also has a path of achieving those promises. I know for me personally, I could have spent more time on my writing (even though I have already spent 10's of thousands of hours), but I would have compromised my time with God and my family. I could have spent more money marketing, but I want to be a good steward of the resources God has given me. I could have knocked on the door of every publisher, agent and editor I could find, but God led me to the few people He had chosen for me. God is my ultimate victory, and He knows the best path to my mountaintop of promise. I will wait in my Sabbath Rest, giving God my full 6 and nothing more, so Christ can respond to my efforts with His 7.

There is another point that I want to share, but I think I can express it better through a fiction meditation. A fiction meditation is where I take something from the Bible, and I breathe it to life with my imagination. This is an amazing way to really meditate on God's Word. The story below is based on Caleb's daughter, Acsah. God's Chosen People are finally in their Promised Land, and they are securing the land and dividing it up amongst themselves.

Caleb gives Acsah and her husband land, but there is obviously something missing—the Spring of Living Water. Acsah goes to her father and pleads for the upper and lower springs, which in essence means the fullness of the water. How smart she is and what an example for us she makes. We can reach our Promised Land without Christ, but a land without Living Water is useless. We can't produce an eternal crop for the Lord without His presence in our Promised Land. When I fully understood that my Promised Land was useless without the Spring of the Holy Spirit, I began to pray desperately for the Holy Spirit to be a wellspring in everything that I do.

> *"A church in the land without the Spirit is rather a curse than a blessing. If you have not the Spirit of God, Christian worker, remember that you stand in somebody else's way; you are a fruitless tree standing where a fruitful tree might grow." – Charles Spurgeon*

The Upper and Lower Springs

A Fiction Verse Meditation

"She answered, 'Give me a blessing; since you have given me land in the South, give me also springs of water.' So he gave her the upper springs and the lower springs" (Joshua 15:19 NKJV).

The Daughter fell to her knees after both of her feet landed in her Promised Land. She wiped the sweat from her brow, unknowingly smudging her forehead with the dirt gathered on her palms from her long journey. Strands of her bound hair slipped across her face and stuck to her damp skin. She tried to sweep them behind her ears, noticing for the first time her muddied hands.

She lifted the corner of her garment and wiped off her fingers. Then she lifted the other corner and rubbed it across her face. Her salted tears mixed with sweat stung her eyes, but she no longer cared about the price to her appearance. The sweat, scars and mud clinging to her body were physical evidence of her climb—a climb that doubled as an inward battle, preparing her to firmly grasp her destiny. The Daughter had become a Warrior. She had persevered, and now she walked into her victory.

Her breaths came heavy, but she paid little attention to her heart pounding inside her wearied frame. She got back onto her feet and made slow steps along the perimeter of her land. She was here. She was home. Her acreage spread across the horizon, but she knew it continued past the rising sun. Her Father promised her this land. A woman, a daughter, a warrior, a steward of her Father's estate—she would not let Him down. She had underestimated the weight of her request, but after years of striving, she had strength to carry the burden of the blessing He bestowed.

As she mentally charted the landscape, a low wave of fear swayed in her stomach. Something was very wrong. She eyed the rising hills shrouded in a sea of green grass—perfect. She glimpsed the grouping of solid trees providing shade—ideal. She reached down and dug her cleaned fingers into the earth and pulled up rich, black soil—unsullied. The land was more beautiful than she could have imagined. Her Father had given her everything she asked of Him.

She scanned the terrain, searching for the reason of her uneasiness. Her breath halted and her eyes darted in desperation, and the full weight of reality knocked her legs back several steps until she collapsed onto her knees. A current of grief poured out of her soul in the form of a despairing moan, and she plowed her hands deep into the ground. Her head dropped onto the grassy floor, and tears fed the parched land of promise until she too thirsted.

The vastness swallowed her tapered cries; and the hills, grass and trees awaited the result of her response. She raised her head and brought her empty hands to her face. She smeared the last of the black soil across her cheeks and sat back onto her heels. A worn but determined expression lined her features, as she struggled back onto her feet. She turned her fixed body toward the overshadowing sun rising in expectation, and she whispered her reply to the attentive ears of the moving wind.

"I forgot to ask for a Spring," she said. "But I'm willing to go back and fight for it." The Daughter stood resolutely with her rigid shoulders squared for battle, and she tried to forget the sacrifices of a thousand yesterdays and prepare for the cost of an endless tomorrow. She would have to leave her Promised Land to find her Father, and He would show her where her next climb began. As she turned to leave, she heard the crackling of a thunderbolt and the rumbling of the atmosphere. Thick, grey clouds blanketed the heavens and the Force of Purpose squeezed the sky.

A river rolled like a mighty tidal wave across the

darkened skyline, and an inverted torrent engulfed the Daughter's waterless field. Saturated pools collected around the roots of trees, across the bottoms of hills and in the dips of pastures; and the rich soil flowed evenly across the expanse. The Daughter lost count of the miraculous forming Springs, and the façade of her determination crumbled, exposing a disillusioned warrior on the verge of defeat.

She fell onto her knees once more. Her legs disappeared under a sparkling layer of liquid. She lifted her face and allowed the water to cleanse the sweat and dirt from her skin. The grimy wounds she tried to ignore eased under the soaking of the rains, and her lips opened to take a drink of the formless water well. The sun stayed hidden behind the stretch of built-up blessings, but she felt His promise rise up within her spirit. As a transparent gust rolled across her emptied body and soul, the cool breeze echoed the unchanging power of her Father's pledge:

> *"When you fight for the Land,*
> *I will provide the Springs."*

"If a spring has not been opened in a soul, a spring of living water from God's own Son, no waters can flow and there is no life in you." – G.V. Wigram

Personal Application

1. Are you waiting for the latter rain to saturate your Promised Land? Have you come to the point where there is nothing else you can do but wait?

2. Have you ever charged ahead, trying to achieve God's will without consulting Him first? Did you feel a lack of His presence in your work?

3. Have you come to the conclusion that no promise is good unless it is filled with the Holy Spirit? Will you pray for God's Spirit to be a wellspring in all you do?

The Promised Land means nothing unless you have the upper and lower springs—the Living Water of Jesus Christ—flowing through it. Your acreage may seem big and beautiful, but without water, the land won't mean much for eternity. The Living Water should be your first priority in all you do. You can ask God for His presence and wait patiently for Him to provide you with not only the land, but with the springs to keep that land fertile and prosperous.

"Father, I want my Promised Land to be rich with the Living Water of Jesus Christ. I want both the upper and lower springs, so I can have fertile soil and produce a continual harvest for You. I pray for You to not only rain down on my land, but for You to fill the land with beautiful springs that flow Your presence into my life and to the lives of the people around me. I pray this in Jesus' name, amen."

Chapter 18

The Great Catch

"Look, I am coming soon, bringing my reward with me to repay all people according to their deeds. I am the Alpha and the Omega, the First and the Last, the Beginning and the End" (Revelation 22:12-13 NLT).

Peter waited all night to catch fish. He was an experienced fisherman. He had his own boat, he had his own net, he had the knowledge and the energy necessary to catch fish, and he seemed to be a leader within the fishermen circles. However, he and his friends fished all night with nothing to show for it. They were exhausted and their human effort left them empty-handed. Many times God will do that in our lives. He will give us His promises, and we will do everything in our strength to make those promises come to fruition. But no matter how hard we work, how many resources we use or how many connections we have, we cannot push our promises into reality. No matter what we do, our 6 will never be acceptable.

But God has a plan as He watches us work all night in seemingly fruitless effort. He has a supernatural "catch" for us to pull up that is so large and so abundant that our nets will tear and our boat will almost topple over with the load. However, he won't give us His 7 until we have spent our 6, got out of our boats and started folding up our nets. God has us wait until we have given up because our strength needs to end before His strength begins. When Jesus saw Peter finishing up for the day, Peter had caught absolutely no fish. All his efforts to bring in a big catch seemed to be futile. But what if they weren't futile.

By trying over and over again, Peter was gaining experience, building stamina and forming better relationships with the people around him. He was giving God all his 6, so he would be better prepared to receive the 7 of Christ. Nothing we do for God is ever in vain. Even if we don't see a harvest in the natural world, the seeds we have planted are hidden in the supernatural just waiting for God to rain down His blessing on them. They will eventually manifest before our eyes. God promises that we will reap what we sow. If we have planted seeds of faith in obedience, our crop is there even if we can't see it just yet. We just need to believe.

> *"The point is this: whoever sows sparingly will also reap sparingly, and whoever sows bountifully will also reap bountifully"* (2 Corinthians 9:6 ESV).

Peter needed to understand that he could do nothing without God involved in all his efforts. Sure, he could make a living and scrape by with a mediocre life, but he could do nothing powerful, eternal or worthy without the saving work of Jesus Christ. Once Peter was done fishing, and his efforts of 6 exhausted, that's when Jesus came with His 7. Jesus was about to take all of Peter's efforts and supernaturally give him a catch that would bring him to his knees before his Savior.

> *"When Simon Peter saw this, he fell at Jesus' knees and said, 'Go away from me, Lord; I am a sinful man!' For he and all his companions were astonished at the catch of fish they had taken"* (Luke 5:8-9 NIV).

I know this to be true for my own life. I spent years and years writing for God, and I always felt like I came up short. I did everything in my 6 to achieve God's promises for me, but my work could never attain God's holy standard. I planted so many seeds of faith without seeing them sprout up that I would have to encourage my faith in God's promises. I knew that my efforts were not in vain. I knew that God had all the seeds that I planted over the years tucked safely in His hands. Even though my work was hidden from the natural world, I trusted that God would eventually unleash His power onto my harvest. I learned to wait in His Sabbath Rest. I learned to be patient for God's abundance. This doesn't mean I sat down idly, doing nothing while I waited for my big catch. On the contrary, I pressed forward, sowing as many seeds as possible in obedience to the Holy Spirit.

Finally, I told God that I needed Him to move on my behalf. I had waited for so many years, believing in His promises, and I desperately wanted to see Him do all the things that I believed by faith that He could do. I had written so many devotionals, articles and stories about God's supernatural power in our lives by faith, but I hadn't really experienced it yet. I longed for the New Wine of Jesus in my life. I wanted Him to rain down His Living Water on my vineyard. I wanted Jesus' Finished Work on the Cross to transform my efforts into an offering pleasing to God. My dreams felt so lost to me that they almost reeked with death. I finally became fed up with my mediocre efforts, and I fasted for a miracle.

In my dryness, my exhaustion and my emptiness, God told me to write this book, but this time I would write it by faith alone. And so I did. I cast my nets and pulled up all the words that I'm writing now. It was not easy and I'm exhausted, but I've been amazed by all the fish that God gave me. I'm in awe of His bounty. I'm honored that He would use me this way. I'm sitting here—ten days after I started writing this book—and every chapter is in my boat. It took a lot of effort and stamina to pull it up, but it is here. I don't know what God will do with it, but I offer my words into the Sabbath Rest of Jesus, so He can transform it into a pleasing offering to the Father.

Now the only thing left to do is wait on God and to lean into His presence. Though we have the revelation of how important it is to rest in the Finished Work of Jesus Christ on the Cross, the process of resting isn't made any easier. We can know the power of waiting in our minds and hearts, but living out that truth is so much more difficult, especially in a society that is all about doing without delay. But I want to be like Jesus' mother, Mary. I want to give Jesus my request and trust that He will come through for me. Waiting in the Sabbath Rest of Jesus is a discipline, which means it will get easier with time and practice. Maybe that is why so many Christian leaders discuss the importance of waiting in their writings—it was a discipline that they too had to learn.

L.B. Cowman wrote accurately in one of her devotionals from *Streams in the Desert*: *"Waiting seems like an easy thing to do, but it is a discipline that a Christian soldier does not learn without years of training. Marching and drills are much easier for God's warriors than standing still."* Standing still in the sovereignty of our great God is an action of faith. In fact, it's the action of abiding in His faithful presence, and it takes "years of training" to get good at it. I know that I still struggle with waiting. Even after everything that God has taught me about Sabbath Rest, I still find myself impatient with God's timing. Hopefully, some day I'll finally learn how to submerge myself completely in Sabbath Rest, and the power of the Holy Spirit will take my efforts and run with them.

> *"I realized that the deepest spiritual lessons are not learned by His letting us have our way in the end, **but by His making us wait**, bearing with us in love and patience until we are able to honestly pray what He taught His disciples to pray: Thy will be done." – Elisabeth Elliot*

Personal Application

1. Have you ever worked all night only to pull up empty nets? Did you struggle with feeling that God had abandoned you?

2. Do you believe that God can provide a supernatural catch in your efforts? Are you willing to patiently wait until Jesus tells you when to cast your nets?

3. Can you obey God's Word without knowing what the end result will be? Do you believe that Jesus can manifest something amazing in your lack if you trust in Him?

God wants to produce something supernatural in your emptiness. He doesn't want you to seek His glory in other things because He's ready to produce His glory within you. He wants to flood your life with His presence, so that the people around you will see His power demonstrated in your life. Trust that God can resurrect the dead and find what was lost. He can do a miracle in your life if you stay yoked to Jesus and stay faithful to His leading.

"God, I want to trust You with my life. I feel empty and alone, but I know that You are there, waiting to pour into my situation. Help me to wait on You. Help me to trust the process of learning to rely on You and learning to abandon myself to Your will. I want You to be a wellspring of Living Water in my life, so I must let go of all my counterfeit sources of nourishment. Today, I submit myself to You and to Your Kingdom plan. I want my life to have meaning beyond this world. I will wait in Sabbath Rest and allow Jesus to manifest His perfection in all that I am and all that I do. I pray this in Jesus' name, amen."

Conclusion

Meet Alisa

"Therefore, since the promise of entering his rest still stands, let us be careful that none of you be found to have fallen short of it" (Hebrews 4:1 NIV).

Today is my 38th birthday. I'm definitely not the same person I was 20 years ago, and by God's grace I will be even better as another 20 birthdays pass me by. I think the most unexpected part of my journey with God is waiting on His promises. I'm sure that Abraham didn't anticipate waiting twenty-five years for his promised son. And surely when Joseph had his dream of being in a position of power, the thought of being a slave and going to jail beforehand never crossed his mind. When David was anointed king, he probably wasn't expecting to wait years and years in the wilderness.

There is a lot of waiting on God throughout all the books of the Bible, and I can personally attest to waiting years for God's promises. In our always busy, productive-focused society waiting has negative undertones. But God has an amazing purpose in waiting, and we must slow down so we can experience the power it produces in our lives.

When God called me to be a writer at age 20, I didn't much care for reading. I was walking into my room in the small house that a college friend and I shared, and God literally spoke over me, "You will be a writer." I remember stopping in my tracks, shrugging my shoulders and saying aloud, "Well, I better start reading then." I wanted to major in kinesiology. I wanted to be a coach, park ranger or physical therapist. I was athletic and enjoyed sports, so sitting at a computer all day wasn't appealing to me.

Finally, I hit my junior year in college and my guidance counselor called me into her office. "You need to pick a major," she said. I had taken all of my core classes, and I dabbled in both English and kinesiology classes. To my amazement, English—especially grammar—started making sense. And my professors saw something special in my writing—something that I couldn't see for myself. After really questioning God's motives for my life, I said goodbye to fun sport electives and physical training classes, and said hello to literature, linguistics and rhetoric. That's when my struggling began. I had to become what I was not. I had to give God my 6, so He could give me His 7.

This book is not about a person becoming a writer; it's about a person giving God all of her efforts and finding sanctuary in His Sabbath Rest. It's about obediently doing everything in the natural and trusting Jesus to take what's offered, so He can unleash His supernatural. God plants our promises as far away as possible, so we can stretch and grow to become people that we never thought we could be. I know this to be true for my life.

I wish I could say that I blissfully went through my waiting time with God, but I can't. I wrestled with God. I questioned Him every step of the way. I was hard on myself, and I never thought to actually enjoy the refining process in my life. I was so work-oriented that I rarely stepped in the rest that God intended for me. I didn't understand that I would never reach my promises without letting go and waiting. It is in the Promise Rest of God that Jesus' Finished Work on the Cross transforms our work into a powerful move of God.

I remember when my first-born son was about 7, and he needed to get a medical procedure done. He fought so hard against the doctor's hands, and afterward, he admitted, "That wasn't so bad." It was so painful to watch him scream and wrestle with the doctor, and I couldn't help but point out how he had wasted so much energy. I exclaimed, "If you would have just trusted the doctor, you would have saved yourself a lot of trouble!" And that's exactly how I look back on my journey to reaching God's dreams for me. If I would have only trusted God and entered into His Rest, I wouldn't have wasted so much energy living in frustration. If I would have only realized that the process I was experiencing was normal, I think I would have been more patient.

I finally found the freedom of entering into God's Sabbath Rest, and I want to share with others the power of waiting on Jesus and relying on His sacrifice. The Blood Jesus shed on the Cross not only forgives us—it frees us from our human striving. Waiting may be one of the hardest disciplines to learn, but it has the most powerful effects on our lives. Join me as I commit to giving God my 6 (the number for humanity and the physical world), so He can faithfully give me His 7 (the number for Sabbath Rest and Jesus' Finished Word on the Cross).

> *"**Waiting** for God is not laziness. **Waiting** for God is not going to sleep. **Waiting** for God is not the abandonment of effort. **Waiting** for God means, first, activity under command; second, readiness for any new command that may come; third, the ability to do nothing until the command is given." – G. Campbell Morgan*

Now that the four cords—the number 6 (our work), the number 7 (His work), Sabbath Rest and the Blood of Jesus Christ have been tightly woven, I pray that the knot of the revelation will free you from human striving and unleash you to enter into God's rest and the Redeeming Work of Jesus Christ. May you make room for Jesus and His Work. Just remember: After our work is done, we rest, so Jesus can do His work!

I hope this book has inspired and touched you as it has me. I pray that you may experience the kindness and goodness of God. May you be blessed by His Son, Jesus, who died to give you everything that He has, including a relationship with our Heavenly Father for eternity.

If you like this book, please write a quick review on [Amazon](). Also, if you enjoy my writing, check out my other non-fiction and fiction works on my website, [www.alisahopewagner.com]().

www.ingramcontent.com/pod-product-compliance
Lightning Source LLC
Chambersburg PA
CBHW060517100426
42743CB00009B/1357